Matthew Hale

Pleas of the crown

A methodical summary of the principal matters relating to that subject

Matthew Hale
Pleas of the crown
A methodical summary of the principal matters relating to that subject

ISBN/EAN: 9783337273309

Printed in Europe, USA, Canada, Australia, Japan

Cover: Foto ©Suzi / pixelio.de

More available books at **www.hansebooks.com**

PLEAS
OF THE
CROWN:
OR, A
Methodical Summary
OF THE
PRINCIPAL MATTERS
relating to that Subject.

By Sir *Matthew Hale*, Knight,
Late Chief Juſtice of the King's Bench.

L O N D O N:
Printed by the Aſſigns of *Richard* and *Edward Atkyns*, Eſquires; for *W. Shrewsbury*, at the *Bible* in *Duke-Lane*, MDCXCIV.

THE PREFACE.

*T*Here was lately Published an Impression, such as it was, of this Book without any Name of Author to it; but yet was commonly given out to have been Written by the late Chief Justice Sir Matthew Hale, and sold for a Book of his Writing. The Original indeed was written by him many years since: But that Impression, as it seems, was, from a surreptitious and very faulty Copy, and was accordingly very Faulty and Corrupt throughout in many respects, what by Omissions not only of Marginal References very frequently, but of many intire Paragraphs, whereby the Book it self is in many places mutilated, as the Reader may easily observe, pag. 19, 23, 48, 52, 57, 108, 110, 122, 183, 187, 200, 202, 203, 208. of that Impression

The Preface.

compared with this, besides divers other shorter, but not less material Notes left out in other places: What by Omissions and Mistakes of single Words, Sentences, and parts of Sentences, and sometimes by an unskilful Critical endeavour to restore to some sense what those Mistakes had made Nonsense, whereby the Sense is in many places maimed and broken, in some much altered, and in some expressed quite contrary to the Author's words and meaning. Instances whereof the Reader may see in pag. 2. lin. 17, p. 4. l. 1. p. 7. l. 6. p. 10. l. 17. p. 14. l. 6. p. 15. l. penult. p. 16. l. 13, &c. the like throughout the whole Book. And what by Transposition of divers matters misplaced among other things to which they have little or no affinity or relation, whereby they are not only wanting in their proper places, but the Order and Coherence of those other Matters among which they are interposed, is interrupted and confounded: Thus one half of the Matter belonging to this Title Process, which should have been continued p. 176, is placed p. 191,

The Preface.

p. 191, 192, 193. *under the Tit.* Pleas, *and the greatest part of the Title* Principal and Accessory, *which should have been continued* p. 196, *is there left off in the midst of a Sentence and placed before at* p. 177. *as if it was the beginning of the Title : and under the same Title four Paragraphs together, which belong to* Accessories after, *and should have been continued* p. 180, *where in the Original they have a connexion with what immediately preceeds and follows, are placed before at* p. 179, *among what belongs to* Accessories before. *Again, the greatest part of what belongs to the Title* Clergy, *and should have been continued* p. 191, *is placed* p. 197, *&c. under the Tit.* Arraignment. *To these might be added other Faults and Mistakes, but these may suffice to shew the general corruption of that Impression.*

And though divers of these Faults and Mistakes are not to be imputed to any Negligence *in the Transcriber or Publisher, (whereof notwithstanding he cannot be acquitted in others) but partly to his* unacquaintance with the

A 3   Au-

The Preface.

Authors hand; *and partly to his Ignorance of his way of Writing, who frequently at the end of his Chapters or Sections used to leave more or less Blank paper, and when other matter occurred, more than could be inserted in those places, did many times write the rest in some other place, where he found most room for it, and for the most part without any Note of reference to it; so that it was very difficult for any, who was not well acquainted with his Writings, to reduce those Transpositions to their proper places; and therefore of the many Copies, which are abroad of this Book, I could never yet see any free from divers such Mistakes; yet by this means (to mention no other) whether through want of Skill, or of Care, or of acquaintance with the Author's Hand and way of Writing, both the Author himself was much injured by the Publication in in that manner, and the Reader also.*

Wherefore to do some Right to the Memory of the deceased Author, and to the Publick, and more particulary in some sort (as far as in respect of

some

The Preface.

some Circumstances was thought fit) *to gratifie the Gentlemen of this Honourable Profession of the Law, who possibly may take it ill to be totally deprived of the benefit of the Writings of so great a Master in it, it was thought good by a Friend of the Authors*, (*whose Care the Author desired in the Publication of his Writings, after his death*) *to furnish the Bookseller with a compleat Copy corrected according to the Author's Original, only what things were therein transposed, were in the Copy reduced to their proper places, according to his Mind.*

To this end it is fit also that the Reader be acquainted, that this Book was Written many years since, about the end of the Reign of King Charles the First, or not many years after; was not by the Author intended for the Press, nor fitted for it; and as he saith in a Letter to one of his Honourable Brethren, to whom he lent it, was then never read over by him since he wrote it, as the Reader may of himself perceive by some Faults, which had escaped him in writing,

The Preface.

and remain uncorrected, as p. 8. l. 22. after the word Dower it is apparent that the word [saved] or some such is wanting (which in the former Impression was endeavoured to be amended, but not without diminution of the Author's meaning) and some others, which are left to the Reader to correct according to his own Judgment, a Method often approved by the most judicious Criticks in the publishing of other mens Writings, and for some special Reasons at this time thought fit to be observed in this.

But lest while we endeavour to do Right to the Author, we should do Wrong to his Book, the Reader must also know, that notwithstanding what hath been said, this Book hath been well accepted and esteemed by divers of the most Eminent Lawyers, who much desired and obtained of the Author himself to have Copies of it many years since. And though probably the Author never at all read it entirely over after he wrote it, yet it is certain he many years after made divers occasional Additions to it: and,

if

The Preface.

f I be not much miſtaken, he did uſually carry it with him in his Circuits.

He hath written a large Work upon this Subject, Intituled, An Hiſtory of the Pleas of the Crown, *wherein he ſhews what the Law anciently was in theſe matters, what Alterations have from time to time been made in it, and what it is at this day. He wrote it on purpoſe to be printed, finiſhed it, had it all tranſcribed for the Preſs in his life-time, and had reviſed part of it after it was tranſcribed; but whether, or when it will be publiſhed is uncertain. In* This *he doth ſummarily relate what the Law is at this time, or rather was when he wrote it, for ſome Alterations it hath ſince received, though not many, by ſome late Statutes; and therefore may not only be of uſe till that be publiſhed, but may alſo continue of good uſe after that is publiſhed, whenever it be, as the moſt proper* Introduction *for Students to this part of the Law that is extant, and as a Synopſis or Epitome of the moſt uſeful part of that.*

A Table

A Table of the Titles, and Method of the Book.

OF *the Kinds of Offences,* pag. 1.
   1. immediately againſt God.
Hereſie, 3.
Witchcraft, 6.
   2. immediately againſt Man.
      1. Capital.
Treaſon,
   High, 9.
   Petit, 23.
Felonies, 26.
   by Common Law.
    1. againſt the Life of Man.
    his own,
Felo de ſe, 28.
    anothers.
      1. Involuntary,
        1. per Infortunium.
Chance-medley, 31.
Deodand, 33.
      2. ex Neceſſitate.
Homicide ex neceſſitate, 35.
   1. *in reference to Publick Juſtice,* 35.
                       2. *upon*

A Table.

    2. *upon Private Interest,* 39.
       Justifiable, ibid.
      Excusable
Se defendendo, 41.
      2. Voluntary.
        1. ex Malitia præcogitata.
Murther, 43.
        2. sine Malitia.
Manslaughter, 56.
    2. against the Goods
Larceny
     1. *Simple,* 60.
     2. *Mixt,* 71.
       1. from the Person,
         putting in fear,
Robbery, 71.
        without putting in fear, 75.
      2. from the House, 76.
  to these may be added
Piracy, 77.
    3. against the Habitation
Burglary, 79.
Arson, 85.
    4. against the Protection of Justice.
Breach of Prison, 87.
  but therein first of
Arrest, 89.

                      Bail,

A Table.

Bail, 96.
   the offence it self
Rumper Prison, 107.
Escape.
   in the Party, 111.
   in a Stranger, 112.
   in an Officer, 113.
Rescue, 116.
Felonies by Statute, 117.
Offences not Capital, 126.
  by Common Law,
    greater,
Misprisions, 1. Negative.
  of Treason, 127.
  of Felony, 129.
  Concealment by Juries, ibid.
  Theftbote, 130.
Misprisions Positive, 131.
Maihem, 133.
Offences not Capital of an inferiour
    nature, 134.
   1. *by an Office.*
Neglect of Duty,
Bribery,
Extortion.
   2. *by a common person*
Breach of Peace,
  1 *Affray*, 135.
              2. *Riot*

A Table.

2. *Riot*, 137.
3. *Forcible Entry*, 138.
   Detainer, 139.
   Restitution, 140.
4. *Barretry.*
5. *Riding armed.*
   Going armed.

Deceipt and Cozenage.
Nusance.
  Publick Bridges, 143.
  High-ways, 144.
  Inns, 146.
  Ale-houses, 147.
Offences not Capital, by Statute, 151.
Forgery.
  Perjury and Subornation, 151.
  Champerty, Embracery, Maintenance, 151.
  Ingrossing, Forestalling and Regrating, 152.
  Matters of Religion, 153.
Proceedings against Offenders, 156.
1. *The Jurisdiction or Court*, ibid.
   The King's Bench, ibid.
   Gaol Delivery, 158.
   Oyer and Terminer, 161.
Justices of Assize, 164.
   of Peace, 165.

Coroner

A Table.

Coroner, 170.
Sheriff, 173.
Court-Leet, 175.
Means of bringing Capital Offenders to trial, 176.
Appeal, 179.
   of Death, 181.
   of Robbery, 184.
   of Rape, 186.
      Court in Appeal, 187.
      Pleas, 189.
Approver, 192.
Indictment, 198.
   Proceedings common to Appeals and Indictments.
Process, 209.
Arraignment, 212.
   Principal and Accessory, 215.
   Arraignment of Principal and Accessory, 221.
Demeanor of the Prisoner, 225.
   Mute, ibid.
     Paine fort & dure, 227.
   Pleas, 228.
     Declinatory.
Sanctuary, 228.
Clergy, 229.

A Table.

To the Felony, 243.
Demurrer, ibid.
Pleas in Abatement.
    Misnosmer, ibid.
  in Bar, 244.
  Auterfoits Acquit, ibid.
    Convict, 247.
  Pardon, 250.
  General Issue, 254.
Trial
  per Patriam, 255.
    Process against Jury, 256.
  Tales, 257.
  Challenge, 259.
  Evidence to the Petit Jury, 262.
  Verdict, 267.
by Battel, ibid.
by Peers, ibid.
Judgments in several Cases, 268.
Falsifying of Attainders, &c. 270.
Execution and Reprieve, 272.

Notes

Notes used by the Author in his References.

C.M.Car. *Coke upon Magna Charta.*
C.West.1. *Coke upon W.1.*
C.PC. *Coke's Pleas of the Crown.*
Com. *Plowden's Commentaries.*
Cr.*and* Crom. *Crompton.*
Dal. *Dalton's Justice.*
Dy. *Dyer's Reports.*
Kel. *Kelway's Reports.*
Lamb. *Lambart's Justice.*
S.PC. *Stamford's Pleas of the Crown.*
4 R. *Coke's fourth Report.*
9 R. *Coke's ninth Report.*

I License this Book to be Printed by *William Shrewsbury.*

18 Mart.
1677.   *Ri: Rainsford.*

PLEAS

OF THE

Crown.

This Treatife (is) divided under thefe Confiderations:
1. Of the *Kinds* of Offences.
2. Of the *Incidents* unto thefe Offences.

The *Kinds* of the Offences are diftinguifhed according to the diverfity of the Laws by which they are introduced, *viz.*

Offences by the Common Law.
Offences by the Statute.

Pleas of the Crown.

Offences *by the Common Law*, diftinguifhed according to the degrees of the Offence.

{ Capital.
{ Not Capital.

Of *Capital* Offences, they are fuch,
1. As are immediately againft God.
2. Immediately againft Man.

Thofe that are Offences *not Capital* by Common Law, as Mifprifions, Maihem, Breach of the Peace, &c.

Offences *by the Stat.* { Capital.
{ Not Capital.

The latter are many, and not here to be treated of.

Herefie.

Heresie.

1. Now first concerning Offences *Capital*, that are *immediately against the Divine Majesty*, which are

{ Heresie,
and
Witchcraft.

1. Concerning *Heresie*, wherein considerable,

I. *What is* Heresie?

At this day all those former Acts which determined certain Points to be Heresie, stand repealed; and though there be no express Act determining what shall be said Heresie, yet the Statute of 1 *El. c.* 1. directing the High Commission, restrains it. [C Pl c.5. St. 1 El.c. 1.]

1. To what formerly determined Heresie, by the Authority of the Canonical Scriptures.

2. To what adjudged so by the first four General Councils.

3. To what expresly adjudged Heresie

Heresie.

Heresie by any other General Council by express words of Canonical Scripture.

4. To what so determined by Parliament by assent of the Convocation.

II. Who to *judge of* Heresie?

1. The Temporal Judge cannot punish any Person for Heresie by Indictment, or otherwise:

But yet incidently he may take knowldge whether a Tenet be Heresie, or not: As where by force of the *Statute* of 2 *Hen.* 4. now repealed, *Kefar* was committed for saying, *That though he were Excommunicate by the Archbishop, he was not so before God:* and *Warner* Committed for saying, *Non tenetur solvere decimas*, and thereupon imprisoned: In a *Habeas Corpus* by the former, and a special Justification in an Action brought by the latter, adjudged neither Heresie.

2. All the *Statutes* that gave power to Arrest or Imprison for Heresie, *viz.* 2 *Hen.* 4. 15. 2 *Hen.* 5. 7. 5 *Rich.* 2. c. 5. 1 and 2 *Ph.*

M. 5 E. 4.
Rot. 143.
coram Rege.

M. 11 H. 7.
R. 327. C. B.

Herefie.

and *Mar. c.* 6. are repealed by 1 *Eliz.*

   III. The way to convict of Herefie.
1. By the Common Law.
    1. By the Archbishops and Bishops in a General Synod.
    2. By the Bishop of the Diocefe.
2. By the *Stat.* 23 *H.*8.*c.*9.

By the Archbishop in cafe of the affent or neglect of his Suffragan.

   IV. The *Punishment* of a Party convict of Herefie.

Upon Certificate of fuch Conviction, a Writ *De Hæretico Comburendo* granted, without which they cannot proceed to any temporal Punishment.

But if after Conviction he abjure his Opinion, his life (is) faved.

But if he relapfe after Abjuration, then irrecoverable.

§. But (by) the *Statute* of 2 *H.* 5. *c.* 7. all *Statutes* which introduc'd any Forfeiture ftand repealed: Neither did the Common Law inflict any Forfeiture, becaufe the proceeding was only *pro falute animæ.*

Witchcraft.

C.P. c.6.

AT Common Law Witchcraft is punished with death, as Heresie, by Writ, *De Hæretico Comburendo.*

The Statute of 1 *Jac.* 12. the only Law now in force against it, and divides it into *two Degrees:*

I. Witchcraft in the *first Degree* made Felony without benefit of Clergy, including *four Species:*

1. *Invocation* or Conjuration of an Evil Spirit.

2. *Consult, covenant* with, *entertain, employ,* feed, or reward any Evil Spirit to any intent, (though no act be done thereupon.)

3. *Take up* any *dead Person*, or any part thereof, to be employed or used in Witchcraft, Charm, &c. (though not actually used or employed.)

4. Exer-

Witchcraft.

4. Exercise any Witchcraft, Inchantment, Charm, or Sorcery, whereby *any Person* shall be *killed*, destroyed, consumed, or *lamed* in his or her Body, or any part thereof (which requires the act to be done, *viz.* laming, consuming, &c.)

These and all Accessary before, to suffer as Felons without Clergy: But Accessaries may be after; but then they have Clergy, because not specially excluded.

II. Witchcraft in the *second Degree*.

1. (To) *take upon them* by Witchcraft, Inchantment, Charm, or Sorcery *to tell where* Treasure is to be found: They that take upon them to do it, though they cannot, yet within this Law.

2. Or where Goods (lost) or stolen may be found.

3. Or to the intent to *provoke* any Person *to unlawful Love*; these Clauses come under the word [*taking upon.*]

Witchcraft.

4. Whereby *Goods or Cattel* shall be *destroyed* (which requires an actual destroying, and not a bare taking upon them.)

5. Or shall use Witchcraft, &c. to hurt any *Person*, though the same be not effected.

The *Punishment* of these,

1. The first Offence, a years Imprisonment and Pillory.
2. The second Offence, Felony. But this requires :
    1. An Actual Conviction and Judgment for the first.
    2. The second Offence must be committed after the Judgment for the first.

The like in Forgery, Transportation of Sheep,&c.

But the Consequents upon an Attainder, *viz.* Corruption of Blood, and loss of Dower: But during life the Lands forfeit.

And Note, a Saving against Corruption of Blood preserves the Descent; and a saving of the Land to the Heir prevents Corruption of Blood.

High

High Treason.

COncerning Offences *against Man* immediately diftinguifhed in their Judgment or Event: Capital, or not Capital.

Capital, either by the Common Law or the *Statutes*; and thefe either Treafon or Felonies.

Treafon, either { High Treafon, or Petit Treafon.

High Treafon: and this though an Offence at Common Law, yet becaufe there be fome mixtures of Introductions of new Treafons by *Statute*, would be confidered together.

1. Confidering High Treafon, it is diftinguifhed into *four kinds*:
    1. That which concerns immediately the King, or his Wife or Children.

High Treason.

2. That which concerns his Officers in the Administration of Justice.
3. That which concerns his Seal.
4. That which concerns his Coin.

Before we come to the Particulars, some things to be generally *premised*.

1. That those that have any such disability upon them, that disables them to act reasonably, cannot commit Treason, *viz. Non compos mentis*, and Infants within the Age of discretion.

And therefore if a Traytor becomes *Non compos* before Conviction, he shall not be Arraigned; if after Conviction, he shall not be executed.

C.P. fo. 4.

An Alien Enemy, committing any hostile act, dealt with as an Enemy: an Alien *amy* committing any Treason, a Traytor within the Law.

2. The *Statute* of 25 E. 3. reduced and setled all Treasons; and by that means all Treasons that were before

High Treason.

before are reduced, and the *Stat.* of 1 *Ma. c.* 1. reinforced the *Statute* 25 *E.* 3. and reduced all new Treasons unto the old Standard of 25 *E.* 3. and so all new Treasons declared between 25 *E.* 3. and 1 *Ma.* abrogated.

3. All Treason includes Felony ; C.Pl.15. therefore if the Indictment want *proditoriè*, a Pardon of all Felonies discharges it.

Now concerning *the kinds* of High Treason.

1. *Compassing* and imagining *the death* of the King, Queen, or Prince, and declaring the same by some open Deed.

I. What (is) a *Compassing* the death?

Declaring by an open act a design to Depose or Imprison the King, is an Overt act to manifest a compassing of His Death.

Calculating Nativity *de Roy nemy* compassing.

II. What a *King* ?

1. A King before his Coronation, a King

High Treason.

a King within this *Statute*, when the Crown defcends upon him.

2. A King *de facto*, and not *de jure*, a King within this Act, and a Treafon againft him punifhable, though the right Heir get the Crown.

3. A Titular King, that is not Regnant; as the Husband of the Queen regnant, not a King within the Act. *Vid.* 1 & 2 *Ph.* & *Ma. c.*10. but the Queen is.

4. The right Heir to the Crown yet not in Poffeffion thereof, is no[t] a King within the Act.

III. What the *King's Wife* ?

It extends not to a Queen Dowager.

IV. What the *eldeft Son and Hei*[r] of the King within the Act[?]

The fecond Son, after the deat[h] of the eldeft, within the *Stat.*

The eldeft Son of a Queen Reg[-]nant within the *Statute*.

The Collateral Heir apparent, a[s] *Roger Mortimer*, 11 *R.* 2. the Duk[e] of *Tork* 39 *H.* 6. not Son and Hei[r] within this Act.

V. Wha[t

High Treason.

V. What an *Overt act* requisite to make such compassing Treason?

1. An Overt act must be alledged in every such Indictment, and proved.

2. Compassing by bare words is not an Overt act, as appears by many temporary *Statutes* against it: 26 *H*.8.*c*.13. 1 *El*.*c*.6. 13 *El*.*c*.1. 14 *El*. *c*. 1, *&c*. but the same set down by him in writing is an Overt act.

3. Conspiring the death of the King, and providing Weapons to effect it, or sending Letters to second it; assembling People to take the King into their power; Lord *Cobham*'s Case; writing Letters to a Foreign Prince inciting to Invasion; an Overt act.

4. Conspiring to levy War no Overt act, unless levied, because it relates to a distinct Treason.

II. Treason *levying War* against the King.

1. A conspiring or compassing to levy War, without a War *de facto*, no Treason; but if a War levied, the Conspirators Traytors as well as

High Treason.

as the Actors: This appears by the *Stat.* 13 *El. c.*1. that made such Conspiracy to levy War, Treason during the Queens life.

2. A raising a Force to burn or throw down a particular Inclosure, only a Riot; but if it had been to go from Town to Town, and cast in all Inclosures, *Bradshaw*'s Case; or to change Religion, or to inhance the Salaries of Labourers, a levying of War, because the End publick.

3. Joyning with Rebels *pro timore mortis, & . recesserunt quam cito potuerunt,* no levying War. *Oldcastle*'s Case.

4. Holding a Fort or Castle against the King's Force, a levying of War.

III. Treason *Adhering to the King's Enemies*, giving them Aid within the Land and without.

1. What *Adhering?*
 1. Giving Aid and Comfort to them.
 2. Surrender the King's Castle for reward.

2. What

High Treason.

2. What an *Enemy*?

1. The Subject of the King becoming a Rebel, he that out of the Realm succours him, this not adhering to an Enemy within this Clause.

2. An Enemy coming hostilely into *England*, shall be dealt with as an Enemy, executed by Marshal Law, or ransomed; but a Subject assisting him shall be dealt with as a Traytor.

3. The *Scots* invading *England* in the Queens time adjudged Enemies, though *Scotland* then in Amity. Lord *Herri*'s Case.

3. *Within the Land* or without, how that Foreign Treason shall be tried.

 1. At Common Law for a Foreign Treason, the Indictment and Trial must be where the Land lies.

 2. By the *Stat.* 35 *H.* 8. *c.* 2. Dy. 298. which is yet in force, it may be inquired of and tried in *B. R.* or by Commission in any County where

where the King appoints; the King's Signature may be either to the Commiſſion o the Warrant thereof.

Treaſon done in *Ireland* is within that *Statute, Perrot*'s Caſe.

Trot. Ab. p. 382.

3. By the *Stat.* 28 *H.* 8. *c.* 15 Treaſon upon the Sea inquirable and triable by Commiſſion in any County; at Civil Law it muſt be befor Lord Admiral.

IV. Treaſon, *Violation* of

1. The King's Wife, extends no to a Dowager.

§. If ſhe conſent 'tis Treaſon i her.

2. The Prince's Wife.

§. The ſame Law as before.

3. The Kings eldeſt Daughter the living.

Thus far of Treaſons that relat to the King's Perſon and neareſt Relations, wherein generally,

1. There muſt be an Overt act t manifeſt that Offence.

2. That muſt be made appear b manifeſt Proof, and not by conjectures.

3. H

3. He must be lawfully attaint thereof, either by Confession, or by his Peers in his life time.

And therefore if a Person be slain in open War he forfeits nothing, neither can he be attaint in such case, but by Parliament.

2. Thus far of Treasons relating to the King immediately; now follows that which is *Interpretative Treason.*

§. *Killing* the Chancellour, Treasurer, Justice of one Bench or other, Justice in Eyre, or of Assize, or Oyer and Terminer in their place, doing their Offices.

1. This *extends* but to the Persons here named, not to the Lord Steward, Constable, or Marshal, or Lords of Parliament.

2. It extends to these only doing their Office.

3. It extends only to a killing, not a wounding without death.

But by *Stat.* 3 *H.* 7. *c.* 14. compassing to kill the King, or any of his Council, made Felony.

High Treason.

3. *Counterfeiting* the Great Seal, or Privy Seal.
   1. It must be an actual Counterfeiting: Therefore compassing to do it, no Treason.
   2. Affixing the Great Seal by the Chancellor without Warrant, no Treason.
   3. Fixing a true Great Seal to another Patent is a great Misprision, but not Treason; nor a Counterfeiting within this *Statute*, 2 *Hen.*4. 25.
   4. Aiders and Consenters to such Counterfeiting are within this Act.
   5. The Counterfeiting of the Privy Signet or Sign Manual not Treason within this Act, but made so by the *Statute* of 1 & 2 *P. M.* c. 11.

V. Treason

High Treason.

V. Treason concerning the *Coin*.

1. *Counterfeiting* the King's Coin. This was Treason at Common Law, but yet the Judgment was only as in case of Petit Treason; this being but affirmance of the Common Law. Vide, Si Mr. de Mint fait memi allay,&c. est Treason. 3 H.7.20.

But whereas *Clipping,&c.* is made High Treason by subsequent *Statutes*, the Judgment is to be hang'd, drawn, and quartered, because introductive of a new Law.

Herein considerable:

1. What shall be a *Counterfeiting?* Clipping, Washing, and Filing of Money for lucre or gain, any of the proper Money of the Realm; or of other Realms, allowed to be current by Proclamation, not Within this *Statute*, but made High Treason by *Stat. 5 El. cap. 11.* but no corruption of Blood, or loss of Dower.

Impairing, Diminishing, Falsifying, scaling or lightening the proper Money of this Realm, or the Money of any other Realm made

High Treason.

made current by Proclamation, their Counsellors, Consenters and Aiders within neither of the former, but made Treason by the *Stat*.of 18 *El*. 1. but without corruption of Blood, or loss of Dower.

2. What his *Money*?
This extended only to the proper Money of this Realm:
But now,

> 1 *Ma. c.* 6. Forging or Counterfeiting Money made *current* by Proclamation, is High Treason.
>
> 14 *El. c.* 3. Forging of Foreign Coin, *not current* here; Misprision of Treason in the Forgers, their Aiders and Abettors.
>
> And Note, The *bare forging* of the King's Coin, without uttering, is Treason. 6 *H:* 7. 13.

Mes uttering de faux Money fait deins le Realm sciant ceo destre fals est solment Misprision de Treason, 3 H. 7. 19. *Issint Receiving, Aiding, &c. cestuy que ad counterfeit,* Dyer 296.

Nota,

High Treason.

Nota, Est grand Misprision, mes nemy Misprision de Treason, & issint resolve 1661.

2. The second offence concerning Money declared Treason, is, if any Person *bringing into the Realm* counterfeit Money.
　1. It must be Counterfeit.
　2. Counterfeit to the similitude of *English* Money.
　3. Brought from a Foreign Realm, and therefore not from *Ireland* barely.
　4. Brought knowingly.
　5. Brought in, and not barely uttered here: But if false or clipt Money be found in his hands, by the Statute *De Moneta*, if he be suspicious, he may be arrested till he have found his Warrant.
　6. He must merchandize therewith, or make payment thereof.

Certain High Treason made by subsequent Statutes in force.

5 *El.* c. 1. Refusing Oath of Supremacy upon the second tender, Treason, without corruption of Blood.

Extolling power of Bishop of *Rome* Premunire, 13 *El.*2. *c.* 2. Bringing in Bulls, or putting in execution, or reconciling to the See of *Rome* thereby, Treason.

Bringing in *Agnus Dei,&c.* Premunire, 1 *El.c.*1. Vide *Dyer* 282.

§. 23 *El. c.* 1. Absolving Subjects from Obedience, or reconciling them to Obedience of *Rome :* Treason in Reconciler and Reconciled.

§. 27 *El.* 2. Priest coming into the Realm, not submitting in two days, Treason. The like for *English* in foreign Seminaries.

Petit

Petit Treason.

IS confined by *Stat.* 25 *E.* 3. to three *Particulars* :
1. Where a *Servant kills* his Master.

This extends to some other Cases:
1. Servant kills his Mistress.
2. Servant kills his Master's Wife.
3. Where a Servant, upon Malice taken during his Service, kills his Master after departure from his Service.

2. *Wife killing* her Husband.

If the Wife and a Stranger kill the Husband, petit Treason in the Wife, Murther in the Stranger.

If the Wife or Servant procure a Stranger to kill her Husband or Master, the Procurer Accessary only to Murther:

Petit Treason.

der: But if she procure a Servant to do it, Treason in both.

3. *Ecclesiastical Person*, Secular or Regular, kills Superiour.

Note, Aiders and Abetters, and Procurers to Petit Treason are within this Act.

V.C.P. 20.
Crom. 18.
Dal.c.91.H.
5 Car. Doddington's Case.

This Act not taken by Equity.

Yet Son kills Father or Mother, it is Petit Treason, receiving Meats, Drink, or Wages.

The *Judgment* in Petit Treason, for a Man to be hang'd and drawn.

Crom. 18. A Woman to be burnt.

Whatsoever will make a Man guilty or principal in Murther, will make a Man guilty or principal in Petit Treason.

Dal. 1.91. But if the Servant kill the Master upon a sudden falling out, this is not Petit Treason, but Manslaughter.

Crom. 19.
Rigg's Case.

If the Servant or Wife be of Confederacy to kill the Husband or Master, and be in the same House, though not in the same Room, they are principals and guilty

Petit Treason.

ty of Petit Treason, for it is a presence.

 Servant tue Mr. per procurement le Feme absent: Il est Petit Treason in Servant, & Accessory al Petit Treason in Feme. 2. *Si Estr. fait ceo per procurement Feme ou Servant: est Murder in l' Estr. & Accessory al Murder in Feme ou Servant.* 3. *Si Estr. fait ceo per procurement & in presence de Feme ou Servant: est Pet. Treason in Feme ou Servant, & Murder in l' Estr'*, Dy. 128, 254, 332.

Of

Of Felonies: And, 1. *Of Felonies of the Death of a Man.*

THus far of High and Petit Treason.

Now for Felonies, they are either: by Common Law, or by Statute.

Felonies *by Common Law:* And they are of four *kinds:*

1. Such as are committed against the Life.

2. Such as are against the Goods of a Man.

3. Such as are against the Habitation of a Man.

4. Such as are against the Protection of Publick Justice.

Felonies committed *against the Life,* of two Natures.

1. That which is committed against his own Life, *Felo de se.*

2. Committed against anothers Life:

   1. Involuntary.

1.*Per*

Felonies.

1. *Per infortunium*, and therein of *Deodands*.
2. *Per necessitatem.*
In defence of Justice.
In defence of self.
2. Voluntary, without Malice.
With Malice.

Felo De Se.

1. **The** *Person.*
    1. As in other Felonies, so in this, the Person that commits it must be of age of discretion, and *Compos mentis*; otherwise no Forfeiture: Therefore if a Lunatick, during his Lunacy, a Man distract by force of Disease, or *Non compos*, kill himself, no Felony.
    2. As in other Felonies, the death must ensue within a year and a day after the stroke, &c.
2. The *Act* may be voluntary. Involuntary in some cases.

St. P. C. 16.
Dalt. c. 92.

If *A.* assault *B.* and *B.* falling down with his Knife drawn, *A.* in pursuit to kill, *B.* by haste falleth upon the Knife, *A.* is *Felo de se*, and forfeits his Goods.

But

But if *B.* were standing in his Defence with his Knife drawn, *A.* runs upon the Weapon and kills himself, *A.* is not *Felo de se*.   C.P.C. p.14.

3. The *Conviction*.
  1. If the Body can be seen, then the Conviction before Coroner, *super visum Corporis*, and not traversable.
  2. If not seen, then before the Justices of the Peace, and then traversable by the Executor or Administrator.   C.P.C. 55.

In the same manner, if enquired n *B. R.* in the same County, traversable.

4. The *Forfeiture:*
  1. When? By the Conviction.
  2. How relating? To the stroke.

Therefore, Villain gives himself a mortal stroke; Lord seiseth Goods; Villain dies; King shall have them.

  3. Of what?

Joint things intire, all forfeited, unless in case of Merchants.   C.P.C. 55.

Joint things severable, Moiety forfeit.

But

But Joint Chattels in Husband and Wife, all Forfeit for this Offence of Husband.

Chance

Chancemedley.

FElony for the death of another, either involuntary, or voluntary.

Involuntary *per infortunium*;
Ex *necessitate.*

Involuntary *per infortunium,* *Chancemedley*, where a Man doing a lawful act, without intent of hurt to another, and death casually ensues:

As, shooting at Rovers, or at a Bird, or hewing a Tree, and the Hatchet-head flies off.

A School-Master in reasonable manner beating a Scholar, or Father his Son, or Master his Servant. Cr. 26.

Doing a lawful thing that may breed danger, and giving warning; Justing by command of the Prince.

But if the Act be unlawful, then death ensuing, Manslaughter or Murther.

Shooting at a Deer in anothers Park, the Arrow glanceth and killeth a stander-by, Manslaughter. C.P.C.56.

Throw-

Chancemedley.

Throwing stones, or shooting in the High-way, and death ensuing, Manslaughter.

G. P. C. 57. But if a Man, knowing People passing by in the Street, throw a stone over the Wall, Murther.

Dalt.c.96. Playing at Hand-sword, without command of the King, death ensuing, Manslaughter.

So that an unlawful act, without an ill intent, Manslaughter; with an ill intent, Murther.

S.P.C.c.15. And this causeth forfeiture of Goods; but a Pardon of Course upon the Special Matter found.

Deodand.

Deodand.

But there is a Death *per infortunium*, without the default or procurement of another: Fall from a Tree, or by a Horse or Cart; and there the thing that occasions the death is Forfeited and *Deodand*: Wherein confiderable,

    1. *What Forfeited* as a Deodand.

    1. If a Man fall from a Cart, or from a Ship in Fresh water, it is a Deodand: Otherwife in Salt water. C. PC. 52.

    2. If an Infant under fourteen be slain by fall from a Cart, Horse or Mill, no Deodand; but if slain by a Horse, Ox, or Bull, then a Deodand.

    3. If a man kill another with any Sword, a Deodand. Dalt. Inst. c. 97.

    2. *When* Forfeited, *viz.*

When found by Inquifition, therefore the Jury ought to find Dalt. c. 97.

Deodand.

the price; and this is before Coroner.

3. The *Relation* of the Forfeiture is to the stroke.

Homicide.

Homicide ex Necessitate.

This of several sorts:
1. In reference to Justice.
2. In defence of his Person, House, Goods.

Homicide *ex necessitate.*

§. 1. *In reference to Justice*, of several kinds:
1. In execution of Justice.
2. In advancement of Justice.

Homicide *in execution of Justice* requires certain Prescripts.

1. That the Judgment be given by one that hath Jurisdiction in the Cause.

If a Justice of Peace give Judgment in Treason, the Execution thereof Murther in Judge and Officer. <small>Dal c.98.</small>

But if he give Judgment of death in Trespass, Felony in the Judge, but not in the Officer that executes it.

2. That it be done by a lawful Officer.

Therefore, if a Stranger of his own <small>Dalt.c.98.</small>

own head, or the Judge that gives the Judgment, Execute it, where it is to be done by the Sheriff, Felony.

3. That it be done purfuant to the Judgment.

S.PC.c. 4. Judgment to be hang'd, Sheriff beheads him, Felony.

2. Homicide *in advancement of Juſtice* in Caufes,

{ Criminal.
{ Civil.

1. In Caufes *Criminal*.

Dalt.c 98. If a Sheriff or Bailiff, having warrant to arreft a Perfon indicted of Felony, and he will not obey, or fuffer himfelf to be arrefted, the Bailiff kills him, no Felony.

Cro. fo. 27. The fame, if any Perfon that purfues upon Hue and Cry, or otherwife to arreft a Felon that flies.

C.PC 22. If a Felon arrefted break-away from his Conductors to Gaol, they may kill him, if they cannot otherwife take him.

But

But in this latter Case there must be a Felony done.

If a Prisoner assaults his Gaoler, and he kill the Prisoner, no Felony.

Rioters, or Forcible Enterers or Deteinors, standing in opposition to the Justice's lawful Warrant, and one of them slain, no Felony.

Keeper or Parker may kill Hunters, if they fly or defend themselves. Cro. fo. 28.

𝕮𝖍𝖆𝖒𝖕𝖎𝖔𝖓 𝖎𝖓 𝖇𝖋𝖊 𝖉𝖊 𝕯𝖋𝖙, 𝖔𝖚 𝕮𝖔𝖒𝖇𝖆𝖙𝖆𝖓𝖙 𝖎𝖚 𝕬𝖕𝖕𝖊𝖑𝖊, excuse in killing the other.

2. In *Civil* Causes.

Though Sheriff cannot kill a man who flies from the execution of a Civil Process, yet if he resist the arrest, the Sheriff or his Officer need not give back, but may kill the Assailant. C.Pl.c.56.

§. So if in the arrest and striving together, the Officer kill him, no Felony.

D 3 Now

Homicide ex Necessitate.

Now touching all the former Homicides, these *things observable*:

1. There must be no Malice coloured under pretence of necessity; for if it be, it alters the Case, and makes it Murther.
2. The Party that did the Fact must be arraigned, and upon *Not Guilty* pleaded, the Special Matter must be found.
3. Upon this Special Matter thus found, the party is to be dismist without any forfeiture or pardon purchased.

2. Thus of Homicide *ex necessitate*, in reference to Publick Justice: Others there are that are grounded upon *Private Interest*, and they of two kinds:

1. *Justifiable*, and consequently inducing no forfeiture at all, nor needing pardon.

2. *Excusable*, and yet inducing a forfeiture.

1. *Justifiable*, and inducing no forfeiture, where a Person comes to commit a known Felony.

   1. If a man come to burn my House, and I shoot out of my House, or issue out of my House and kill him, no Felony. Dalt.c.31.

   2. If a Woman kill him that assaulteth to Ravish her, no Felony.

   3. If Thieves assault me in the High-way, or in my House to rob me, and I, or my Servant kill them, no Felony nor forfeiture. 24 H.8.c.5.

D 4   But

But if the Assault in my House were not to rob me, but to beat me, &c. there would be only *se defendendo*, and Goods forfeited, and a Pardon of course to be granted, because (they) came not to commit a known Felony ; for it cannot be judged whether he meant to kill me.

Dalt. c. 98. If one come to enter into my House, claiming Title, and I kill him, Manslaughter.

Crom. 24. If *A.* enter wrongfully into the House of *B.* riotously and forceably, *B.* and others endeavour to fire the House, *A.* kills, Manslaughter.

Se defendendo.

Homicide *Excusable Se defendendo*, which though it save the Life, yet the Goods are forfeited; this requires these things:

1. It must be an inevitable necessity. C.PC.f.56.

In case of a justifiable Homicide, as of a Thief that comes to rob me, or by an Officer resisted in Executing an Arrest, the Party need not give back to the Wall.

But in this Homicide *Se defendendo*, the Party that is assaulted not excused, unless he give back to the Wall. C.PC. 57.

But if the Assault be so fierce, and in such a place that giving back would endanger his Life, then he need not give back. C. PC. 57.

A man fights, and falls to the ground, then flying not necessary. Dalt c.98.

2. It must be in his defence.

If *A.* be assaulted by *B.* and before a mortal Wound given, *A* gives back till he come to the Wall, and then C.PC. 56.

then in his defence kill *B.* this is *Se defendendo.*

But if the Mortal wound firſt given, then Manſlaughter.

<small>Dalt. c.98. Crom. 26.</small>

If *A.* upon Malice *præpenſe* ſtrike *B.* and then fly to the Wall, and there in his own defence kills *B.* this is Murther.

But if there be Malice between *A.* and *B.* and *A.* ſtrike firſt, *B* retreats to the Wall, and in his own defence kills *A.* this is *Se defendendo.*

<small>Cro. fo. 25.</small>

If Malice be betwixt *A.* and *B* and *A.* aſſaults *B*. *B.* retreats to the Wall, and then kills *A.* in his own defence; if it be in the High way he ſhall be diſcharged, but if not, yet it is *Se defendendo. Copſton's Caſe.*

Murther.

Murther.

Thus far of Homicide Involuntary.

Homicide *Voluntary* is either:

Ex malitia præcogitata, which is *urther*.

Sine malitia, Manslaughter.

Murther is, when a perſon killeth other of malice within any County England, ſo he dye within a year d a day.

. Who ſhall be ſaid a *perſon-killing*?

A Man that is *Non compos* kills Dalt. other, this is no Felony.

§. The ſame for a Lunatick, during s Lunacy.

But he that incites a *Mad-man* to ll another, is a principal Mur-erer.

A man *drunk* killeth another, this Felony.

An *Infant* within age of diſcretion lls a man, no Felony; as if he be or 10 years old.

But if by circumſtances it appear-
eth

eth he could diſtinguiſh betwee[n] Good and Evil, it is Felony: As [if] he hide the dead, make excuſe, &c.

<small>Crom. 27.</small>

But in ſuch caſes, Execution i[s] prudence reſpited to obtain a Pa[r]don.

<small>St.PC.c.9.</small>

2. What ſaid *Malice*?

It is either implied or expreſſed.

Implied Malice is collected eithe[r] from the manner of doing, or fro[m] the perſon ſlain, or from the perſ[on] killing.

1. Malice implied *in the mann[er]* of doing.

Poyſoning wilfully any man, im[-]plies malice.

<small>C.PC.52.</small>

If a man do an act that apparen[t]ly muſt introduce harm, and deat[h] enſue; as to run among a multitud[e] with a Horſe uſed to ſtrike.

<small>Dalt.c.93.</small>

But Note, That if it were with a[n] intention to do harm, then Mu[r]ther; if without ſuch intention, Man[-]ſlaughter.

The like of throwing a Ston[e] over a Houſe among many People, the intention of doing harm make[s]
it

Murther.

Murther; want of such intention, manslaughter, because the act unlawful.

For an intention of evil, though not against a particular person, makes malice.

Killing any person without provocation, Murther.

A. comes to rob B. B. resists and strikes, A. kills him, Murther.

A. Distorts his mouth and laughs M.42,43 El. B. who thereupon kills him, Mur- *Brame's* case. ther.

2. Malice implied *in respect of the person killed*.

If a Watchman or Constable, or 4 R. Hamd. any that comes in his assistance, doing case, *Young's* their Office, be killed, it is Murther, case. though the Killer knew him not to be such.

If any Magistrate or Minister of Justice, having a lawful Warrant, be killed, doing his Office, it is Murther: as where a Serjeant comes to Arrest,

    1. Though in the Night.
    2. Though on Sunday.
    3. Though upon the Arrest
                              he

he shew not out of wh
Court, or whose Suit.

9 Rep. Mac-kally's Case.

4. Though the Proces Err
neous.
5. Though he shew not h
Warrant or Mace, where it
not demanded.

But if the Officer do what is n
warrantable, as break open a Windo
to Arrest, there though slain, Ma
slaughter only. *Pasch. 15 Car. Cool
Case.*

Malefactors come into a Parl
the Parker shoots, they fly, he pu
sues, they kill him, Murther in al
for their first entry was with
Malicious intent. *Mich. 17 Jac. Usrai
Case.*

3. Malice implied *in respect of t.
person killing.*

A. assaults *B.* to rob him, *B.* resist
A. kills him, Murther.

Prisoner by Duress of the Gaol
comes to an untimely end, Mu
ther.

Executing Martial Law in time
Peace, Murther.

2. Mali

2. Malice *Express* confiderable,
   1. In the Principal in the firſt degree, that doth the act.
   2. In the Principal in the ſecond degree, that is preſent and aiding, or abetting.
   3. In the Acceſſory before the Fact.

I. In the Principal *in the firſt degree.*

1. If a perſon have no particular Malice againſt any Special perſon, but comes with a general reſolution againſt all Oppoſers, if the act be unlawful, and death enſue, it is Murther: As if it be to commit Riot, to enter into a Park; Lord Dacre's Caſe. Crom. 20.

2. If there be Malice between *A.* and *B.* and they meet and fight upon that Malice, though *A.* gives firſt blow, yet if *B.* kill him, it is Murther. Crom. 21.

If there be Malice between *A.* and *B.* and *A.* aſſault *B.* and after *A.* flies to the Wall, and there in his own defence kill *B.* by ſome this is Murther; but *Quære.*

If there be quarrel between *A* and *B*. and *A*. challenge *B*. *B*. declines it; but at length upon Importunity and to vindicate his Reputation meets and fights, and kills *A*. this is Murther, *Pasch.* 14 *Jac. Taverner*'s Case.

If *A*. and *B*. fall out upon a sudden and they presently agree to fight and each fetch a Weapon and go into the Field, and one kills the other C.PC. 55, 57. this is only Manslaughter, because the Blood never cooled: but otherwise if they appoint to fight the next day.

Laurence case. *A*. and *B*. fall out, *A*. saith he will 38 *El.* not strike, but will give *B*. a pot of Ale to touch him, *B*. strikes, *A*. kills him, Murther.

If *A*. and *B*. are in Malice, and *A*. challenge the Field, and *B*. refuse to meet, but he saith he shall go to morrow to such a Town, *A*. meets him, assaults him, and *B*. kills him Manslaughter, and no Murther.

H:ll. 9 *Jac.* The Child of *A*. beats the Child *Rawly's* case. of *B*. who runs home to his Father and he runs three quarters of a mile beats

beats the other Child, and he dies; Manflaughter.

3. If Malice be not continuing till the death, no Murther.

A. and *B.* combat upon Malice, C_tom. 21. and are parted, and after they meet and combat upon the fudden, and one kills the other; by fome not Murther, becaufe the firft Malice fatisfied.

If the party killed had wounded at the firft combat the party flaying, *Quære*.

A. and *B.* are at Malice, and reconciled, and after upon a new Occafion fall out and kill, no Murther.

4. Though the Malice did *not rife fo high* as death, but intended only to beat the party; yet if malicious, it is Murther if death enfue.

A Keeper of *Efterly* Park finds a Boy ftealing Wood, bound him to his Horfe-tail and beat him, the Horfe ran away, kill'd the Child, Murther; for it was a deliberate act, *Mich.*4 *Car.B.R Holloway's* Cafe.

5. The

5. The malice intended to one, *egreditur personam*, and makes the death of another upon that malice, Murther, and qualifies the act in the same manner, as if it had had its due effect.

Dy.128.   *A.* having malice at *B.* strikes at him, and misseth, and kills *C.* this is Murther in *A.* and if it had been without malice *præpense*, Manslaughter.

Crom.101. Elly's case.   *A.* having malice to *B.* assaults him, and kills the Servant of *B.* this is Murther in *A.*

9 Rep.Gore's case.   *A.* lays poison to kill *B.* and *C.* at misadventure takes it, and dies; Murther in *A.* Contrary, if it had been laid to kill *Rats*; then *infortunium*.

   A. and *B.* combat upon malice, *C.* comes to part them, *A.* kills *C.* this is Murther, and *per ascuns*, Murther in both; and if the falling out were sudden, then only Manslaughter in him that kill'd him. *Vide Dyer* 128. 20 *E.*3.*Corone* 262.

   6. The malice must be of Corporal damage to the party.

2.Prin-

Murther.

II. Principals *in second degree*, that are aiding and abetting.

1. If two or more come together to kill, rob, or beat a man, or to commit a Riot, and one of them kills a man, this is Murther in all them of that party that are present, aiding or abetting him thereunto, or that were ready to aid him; though but lookers on: Otherwise, if he came there by chance. St. PC. c. 40.

2. All are said to be present that are in the same House, though in another Room, or in the same Park, though half a mile distant; and out of view; therefore if they came to commit a Felony, such persons aiding or abetting shall be said present. 34 H. 8. B. *Coron.* 172. M. 17 *Jac. Warnial's* case. *Crom.* 19. Dalt c. 93.

3. *A.* and *B.* fall out, and appoint the Field; *A.* takes *C.* his Second; *B.* takes *D.* his Second; *A.* kills *B.* this is doubtless Murther in *C.* and hath been held Murther in *D.* also, for it is a Compact: But it seems otherwise. Dalt. c. 93. Dy. 128.

4. If *A.* and *B* having malice *præpense*, meet and fight, and *C.* the

E 2   Ser-

Crom.100.

Servant of *A.* not acquainted therewith, take part with *A.* his Master, and kill *B* this is Murther in *A.* but only Manslaughter in *C.*

The same Law if *C.* came in suddenly, and took part with *A.* and kill'd *B. Vide* Sir *Ferdinando Cary*'s Case, 14 *Jac.*

Mes si un vient la per chance, & n'abette, n'est principal, nec accessor: al Manslaughter ou Murther, Stamf. 4º.

3. What Malice in the *Accessor* before the Fact.

A. commands *B.* to kill *C.* with a Gun, he kills him with a Sword *A.* is accessory to this Murther because the killing was the substance.

But if he command *B.* to kill *C* and he by mistake kill *D.* this i Murther in *B.* but *A.* is not accessor thereunto.

A. commands *B.* to beat *C.* wh beats him, whereof he dies, this i Murther in *B.* and *A.* is accessory because death ensues upon the ac commanded.

4. Wha

4. What *Killing?*

Prison, Weapon, Gun, Bow, Crushing, Bruising, Smothering, Strangling, Famishing, inciting Dogs.

§. Laying a Sick man in the cold.

Laying an Infant in an Orchard under Leaves, and he stricken with a *Kite*.

A man keeps a Beast used to strike knowingly, and ties it not up, the Beast kills a Man, Felony by some, by others not, but a great Misdemeanour, 3 *E.* 3. *Cor.* 311. ^{St Dal.c.93.}

5. What the *person killed?*

It must be a person *in rerum natura*.

If a Woman quick with Child take a Potion to kill it, and accordingly it is destroyed without being born alive, a great Misprision, but no Felony; but if born alive, and after dies of that Potion, it is Murther.

The like, if it dies of a stroke given by another in like manner.

§. Counsel before the birth to destroy it, and after the Child is born ^{C.PC.c 7. Dal.c 93. contra.}

E 3

Murther.

Ibid.

born destroyed accordingly, the Counsellor is Accessory.

6. What a place *within the Realm?*

C.PC.c.7.

Stroke and death *in partibus transmarinis* not punishable at Common Law, but before the Constable and Marshal.

Stroke and death upon the Sea inquirable before the Admiral, or according to the *Stat.* of 28 *H.* 8. *c.* 13. But Stroke upon the Sea, and death within the Body of the County, not punishable at all.

If the Stroke in one County, and the death in another, the party shall be indicted where the death hapned.

An Accessory in the County of *A.* to a Felony committed in the County of *B.* the Accessory after Certificate of the Conviction and Attainder of the Principal, may be Arraigned upon an Indictment in the County of *A.* where he was Accessory. *Stat.* 2 *E.* 6. *c.* 24. *Vid. Formam Processus inde in B. R. C.PC. cap* 7. *Overbury's* Case.

7. The

Murther. 55

7. The party muſt die *within the Year and the Day* of that Stroke, or Poiſon, &c.

E 4   *Man-*

Manslaughter.

KILLING another upon a sudden falling out, or provocation, or unjustifiable act, Manslaughter.

1. What a *sudden falling out?*

C. PC. c.8. Two combat and part, and presently come together and fight, or one presently fetcheth a Weapon and killeth the other, or they presently fetch their Weapons, and go into the field, and one kills the other, Manslaughter.

Divers Rioters enter into anothers House forcibly, and eject the People; afterwards they being in possession, the party ejected, with twenty more, come in the Night to the House, endeavour to fire it, and one within shoots and kills one of the assailants; ruled to be Manslaughter, because their entry and holding with force illegal; and not Murther, because a sudden provocation.

Manslaughter.

So *A.* claims Title to the house of *B.* *A.* attempts to enter and shoots at the house; *B.* shoots out and kills *A.* adjudged Manslaughter.

Two fall out and fight, and one breaks his Sword; a Stranger standing by sends him another, and he kills therewith, Manslaughter in both. ^{Dalt.c.94.}

2. What a *sudden provocation*?

Two strive for the Wall, and one kills the other, Manslaughter.

3. What *unlawful act*, whereupon Death ensuing will make Manslaughter?

If the unlawful act be deliberate, and tend to the personal hurt of any immediately, or by way of necessary consequence, death ensuing, is Murther.

But if either such deliberation or intent of personal hurt be wanting, Manslaughter.

Two play at Foils, and one kills the other, Manslaughter. Sir *John Chichester*'s Case, 11 *H*.7. 23. *Vide Kell.* 108, 136. *Wrastling, & un tue autre.*

A.

Manslaughter.

A man throws a Stone at another, which glanceth and killeth another, Manslaughter; and not Murther, because no malicious intent to hurt; not *per infortunium*, because doing an unlawful act.

There is a particular Manslaughter, wherein Clergy is ouft, by the *Stat.* 1 *Jac.c.*8. wherein,

1. He that is ousted of Clergy by that *Statute*, must be especially indicted pursuant to the *Statute*.

2. It extends to him that actually gave the Stroke, not to those that are present.

3. Need not conclude *contra formam Statuti*.

4. Although the Indictment be Special upon the *Statute*, yet the Jury may find general Manslaughter. *Hill.* 23 *Car. B.R. Page*'s Case.

A. Newgat.rep. 16 *Car.* 2. A man whips his Horse in the Street to make him run speedily, and the Horse runs over a Child, and kills him; Manslaughter: But another whips the Horse, whereby he springs out, and runs over a Child, and kills him;
per

Manslaughter.

per infortunium. Nota, *Indictment de Murther per ceo que est per infortun' sur non culp' pled' Jury poet trover luy non culp' si soit Coroners Inquest, que trove ceo per misfortune & le party conust ceo.* **Prettye's Case.**

Larceny.

Larceny.

WE come to Offences Capital, which refer to *the Goods* of any Perſon, *viz. Larceny*, which is of two kinds:

{ Simple Larceny,
{ Mixt and complexed Larceny

Simple Larceny of two kinds:
Grand Larceny, of the value o[f] 12 pence.
Petit Larceny, under that value.

Simple Larceny, a felonious an[d] fraudulent taking away by an[y] perſon of the meer perſonal Good[s] of another, not from the perſon, no[r] out of his houſe, to the value o[f] 12 pence.

I. Wha[t]

Larceny. 61

I. What shall be said a *Felonious taking?* Imports two things:

1. A Taking necessary; the Indictment must be *Cepit*; if it be *felonice Abduxit Equum*, not sufficient.

If a person find Goods lost, and convert them, though the Conversion were *animo furandi*; yet no Felony. C.P.C.

If a man hath a *bare charge* of Goods, Felony may be by him committed: As a Butler that hath charge of Plate, Shepherd of Sheep; the like of him that hath a *bare special use*, as the Guest that hath Plate set before him.

But he that hath a *possession by delivery*, cannot thereof commit Felony.

A Carrier hath Goods delivered to him, and he carries them away, no Felony.

A. lendeth his Horse to a Stranger, who rides away, no Felony.

A Clothier delivers Yarn to a Weaver

Larceny.

Weaver to weave, he carries it away, or imbezels it, no Felony.

But this hath two Exceptions:

1. If the Privity be determined, then it may be Felony.

A. delivers a Pack or a Tun of Wine to a Carrier, he opens it, and take out Goods or Wine, *animo furandi*, Felony.

So if *A.* deliver Goods to *B.* to carry to a certain place, he carries it to the place appointed, and after takes it *animo furandi*, Felony.

2. By *Stat.* 21 *H.* 8. *c.* 7. whereby if a Servant goes away with the Goods of his Master, delivered to him above the value of 40 shillings; herein,

C.PC.c.44.
Dalt.c.102.

    1. Extends not to Apprentice, nor Servants within eighteen years.

    2. Requires a Delivery. If one Servant deliver the Goods to the other, this is delivery by Master.

If

Larceny.

If the Master deliver an Obligation, or deliver Cattel to sell, and the Servant receive the money and depart with it, it is no Felony: The like if he had gone away with the Obligation.

3. He must go away with it. Wastfully consuming, &c. thereof, [n]o Felony.

4. Now by the *Stat.* of 1 *E.* 6. *c.* 12. he may have his Clergy.

5. He must be a Servant at the time of the delivery, and going away; therefore for imbezelling after Master's death, *Stat.* 33 *H.*6 *c.*1. gives remedy.

6. If a Servant receive his Master's Rents, and go away with them, not within the *Statute.*

If a man, seeing a Horse in the [p]asture of the Owner, having a mind [to] steal him, obtains a Replevin, and [th]ereby hath the Horse delivered, [th]is is a Felonious taking. C.PC.57.

If

Larceny.

Crom. 34.
If *A.* felonioufly take my Horfe and *B.* felonioufly takes him from him, *B.* may be appealed or indicted as of a felonious taking from me §. *Stat.*33 *H.*8.*c.*1. Falfe token.

Un prift feme de I. S. *ove fes bien countre le volunt, eft Felony: Contr fi feme prift les biens le baron & al ove eftr' de fa bone volunt.* 13 Aff. (*Iffint fi feme covert prift biens le baroi ou eux dona al eftr' que eux impor. neft Felony.* Abridg. Aff. 63.

II. What a *Carrying away?*

C.PC. c. 47.
A Gueft takes Sheets out of tl Bed, brings them into the Hall wit an intent to carry them away, bi is apprehended before this; a Ca rying away.

A. takes the Horfe of *B.* with a intent to fteal him, but is appr hended before he can get out of tl Pafture; this Taking away.

Crom. 33.
A. kills my Sheep, ftrips them carries away their Skins, Felony; 1 if he pull off their Wool.

III. *l*

Larceny.

III. *By whom?* and who such a person, as may commit Larceny.

An *Infant* under Fourteen years may commit Larceny; but prudence to respit Judgment; yet one under Fourteen burnt in the Hand. *Presidents.* Dalt.104.

A *Feme covert* by her own act may commit Larceny, and in such case the Husband may be Accessory to the Wife in receiving her; but not *è converso*.

But she cannot feloniously take her Husband's Goods; and though she so take her Husband's Goods, and deliver them to a Stranger, yet no Felony in the Stranger.

If Husband and Wife do both a Felony, this is Felony in both, and both arraigned for it. Dalt.104.

Nota, Books old and latter, and Practise, *contra*.

If the Wife commits Murther by coercion of her Husband, Murther in both; but if theft, no Felony in her;

Larceny.

her; but a bare Command excuseth her not.

But if a *Servant* commit Theft by Coercion of his Master, yet it is Felony.

IV. What meer *personal Goods*?

Dalt.c.47.   1. If they are in the Realty, or annexed thereunto, no Larceny: As Corn or Grass growing, Apples on Trees.

§. Stealing a Chest of Charters, no Felony, though the Chest above value.

Taking Lead off a Church no Felony: Otherwise if he leave it a while, and after come and take it.

Taking an Infant Ward, no Felony.

2. If they are of a base Nature, as Mastiffs, Dogs, Bears, Foxes, Monkeys, Ferrets, or their Whelps, there can be no Felony of them; but of Hawks reclaimed Felony may be.

Larceny.

V. What said the *Goods of another*.

1. He that hath a Special property, as a Bailiff, &c. they are his goods *pro tempore*. *A.* bails Goods to *B.* and after to the intent to charge *B.* steals them from him, Felony in *A.* 21 *H.* 7. *Kel.* 70. *Cloth in maines Toylor*.

2. He that takes the Goods of a Chapel in time of Vacation, indictable *quare bona Capellæ*; so *bona Paochianorum*, *bona mortui*, or *bona ignoti*, &c. Dal. 103.

So to steal the Shroud of a Person buried; and it shall be *bona Executorum*. *Vid. Tamen contra*; 15 *Jac.* *Tottingham*'s Case. C. PC. c. 47.

But taking of Treasure trove, Wrecks, Waifs and Strays before seisure, no Felony.

Taking an Obligation Felony, because in action.

Taking Fish in a River no Felony; but Fish in a Net, Trunk, or Pond, Felony, because not at their natural liberty:

Larceny.

liberty: So of old Pigeons out of the House.

Where a man hath a Property only *ratione loci*, or *privilegii*, in things *feræ naturæ*, as Coneys or Deer in my Ground, Park or Warren, no Felony.

Mes fil ne conu-
sant d'estre
tame, n'est Fe-
lony.
V.Mag.Chart.
201.

But if reduced to tameness, and fit for food, as Deers, Coneys, Cranes, Partridge, Pheasants, he that stealeth them, knowing them tame, committeth Felony.

So of Swans marked and pinioned, or Swans unmarked if tame, kept in a Mote, Pond, or private River.

Where a man hath a Property *ratione impotentiæ* in things wild by Nature, as young Hawks in the Nest, young Pigeons in the Nest, Felony thereof.

Taking of Eggs of Hawk or Swan out of the Ground of another, no Felony, but punishable by *Statute*.

But taking any thing *domitæ naturæ*, as Duck, Hen, Geese, Turkeys, Peacoks, or their Eggs; or Domestick

mestick Beasts, as Horses, Mares, Colts,&c. or their young, Felony.

VI. Where this shall be said a *Felonious taking*.

If *A.* steal Goods in the County of *B.* and carry them into the County of *C.* he may be appealed or indicted in the County of *C.* for Larceny, but can be indicted of Robbery only in the County of *B.* Only in the former Case the *Stat.* of 25 *H.*8. *c.*1. ousts them of their Clergy, if they were not to have had Clergy if arraigned in the County of *B.* where the Robbery committed. Crom. 34. V. 4 H. 7. 5.

Si Guest prist Sheets hors de lect feloniously, & eux import in hale, & la sur fear de pursuit relinquish eux, Felony. 27 Ass. 39.

VII. Of the *value* of Twelve pence, or above.

1. *Nota*, That in case of Grand Larceny it must be above the value Westm 1. c.15. 21 Jac c.6.

Larceny.

of Twelve pence; and if it be but of the value of Twelve pence, or under, it is Petit Larceny.

2. If two steal Goods to the value of Thirteen pence, this is Grand Larceny in both.

Dal. c.101.
Crom. 36.
St.PC. c. 24.

3. If one person at several times, at one time steal Four pence, at another Six pence, at another Three pence, in all amounting to above Twelve pence, from the same person, all these put together in one Indictment, amount to Grand Larceny; and Judgment of Death.

4. If a man be Indicted of stealing Goods to the value of Ten shillings, and the Jurors find Specially, as they may, the value but Ten pence, 'tis but Petit Larceny, and no Judgment of Death.

And Note, Petit Larceny is Felony, though not of Death; and for this he shall forfeit Goods, and be subject to Whipping, or other Corporal punishment. *Issint si fugam fecit furt biens.* Coron. 106.

Robbery.

Robbery.

COmplicated or mixt Larceny, which hath a farther degree of guilt in it.
1. For that it is a Taking from the Perſon.
2. For that it is a Taking out of the Houſe.
1. Taking *from the Perſon.*
 1. Where the Perſon is put in fear, and then 'tis Robbery.
 2. When not put in fear, and then 'tis Larceny from the Perſon.

Robbery is a felonious and violent taking away from the perſon of another Mony or Goods to any value, putting him in fear.

1. *Violent and putting* him *in fear*; the words of the Indictment run, *violenter & felonice*, and that diſtinguiſhes him from a Cut-purſe.
 2. *Taking away.*
 1. An aſſault to rob without any taken, is no Felony.

Robbery.

If a Thief, with or without Weapon drawn, bid the party deliver his Purse, and he doth it, this is a taking to make it Robbery.

Crom. 31.

If a Thief command to deliver his Purse, and he deliver, and the Thief finding little in it, deliver it back, this is Robbery.

C. PC. c. 16.

If a Thief compel the True man by fear to swear, to fetch him a Sum of Mony, which he doth accordingly, and the Thief receives it, it is Robbery.

If the True man's Purse be fastned to his Girdle, the Thief cuts the Girdle, the Purse falls to the Ground, no Robbery; but if the Thief take up the Purse, though he let it fall again, Robbery, though he never take it up more.

All that come in Company to rob, Principals, though one only actually do it.

Crom. 34.

A.B. and C. assault D. to rob him in the High way, but rob him not, for that he escaped: A. rides from the rest, in the same High way, and robs E. out of view of the rest, and

came

came back to the rest, and for this *B.* and *C.* arraigned and hanged, though assented not, because they all came to the end to rob. *Pudsey's* Case.

3. Taking *from the Person.*

If the True man, seeking to escape, casts his Purse into a Bush, or let fall his Hat, if the Thief take it, Robbery.

Taking a thing in my presence, is in Law a taking from the Person.

If one take or drive my Cattel Dalt.c.101. out of my Pasture in my presence, this is Robbery, if he make an assault upon me, or put me in fear.

But if he take any thing from my Dalt.ibid. Person, without putting me in fear Dyer 224. by assault or violence, no Robbery; and the Indictment runs, That he took it from the Person violently and Dalt. ibid. feloniously, putting him in fear.

4. Of what *value* soever.

Though under Twelve pence. C.PC. c.16. *Mes in forein County in tiel case petit Larceny, car n'est Robbery la.* : Jac. *More's* Rep.

Now though Robbery and simple

Robbery.

ple Larceny are both Capital, yet they differ in thefe Refpects:

1. The Principal and Acceffory before are oufted of Clergy, but not in Simple Larceny.

§. *Stat.* 23 *H.* 8. *c.* 1. 1 *E.* 6. 12 25 *H.* 8. 3. 4 & 5 *Phil.* & *Ma. c.*4 *Nota,* fpeaks of Robbery in or near the High-way.

2. In the form of the Indictment:

An Indictment of Robbery fuppofeth an Affault, beating and wounding, and taking from the perfon *felonice*; or at leaft affault and putting in fear, *felonice & violenter cepit à perfona*: Other Indictments though of a taking from the perfon yet not *violenter*.

3. In cafe of other Thefts, though from the perfon, not Felony of Death, unlefs it exceed Twelve pence. But here it is Felony of Death never fo fmall.

Larceny

Larceny from the Person.

Larceny from the Person *without putting in Fear*; which may be either by picking the Pocket, or cutting the Purse, which is supposed to be done *clam & secrete à persona.*

In this Case by the *Stat.* of 8 *El.c.*4. the Indictment pursue the *Statute*, which is secretly without the knowledge of the party, *clam & secrete,* he is ousted of his Clergy.

But if it be under value of Twelve pence, then it remains Petit Larceny, as before; for the *Statute* did not alter the Offence, though it took a Privilege. C. PC. c. 8 Crom.103.

Larceny from the Person, which is neither *clam & secrete à persona,* nor with putting in Terror, nor so laid in the Indictment, nor so found by the Jury, Clergy. *Dyer* 224. 17 *Jac. Harman's* Case.

Larceny.

Larceny from the House.

Larceny receives another aggravation, when it is taken *from the Habitation* of a man.

Per Stat.
23 H. 8. c. 1.
Robbing any person in their dwelling-house, the Owner, his Wife, or Children, or Servants being within, and put in fear, ousted of Clergy in case of Conviction, together with Accessories before, by *Stat.* 23 *H.* 8. *c.* 1.

Felonious taking of Goods to the value of Five shillings out of any Dwelling-house or Out-house, tho' no person within, oust of Clergy by 39 *El. c.* 15.

These have a Mark upon them as Larcenies complicated, and so oust of Clergy. *Vide infra Clergy.*

Piracy.

Piracy.

To this we may add Piracy and Depredation upon the Sea.
This at Common Law convicted, C.PC.c.49. Petit Treason, if done by a Subject.

But this alter'd by *Stat.* 25 *Ed.* 3.

Since that *Statute* an Offence trible by the Civil Law till 28 *H.* 8. 5.

The *Stat.* 28 *H.* 8. alters not the Offence; but it remains only an Offence by the Civil Law: and therefore a pardon of Felonies doth not discharge it: but it gives a Trial by the course of Common Law:

1. It extends not to the Accessories: But if the Accessory were at Sea, triable by the Civil Law; if at Land, by no Law: For *Stat.* 2 & 3 *E.* 6. extends not to it.

2. It extends not to Offences in Creeks or Ports within the Body of a County, because punishable by the Common Law.

3. Though

3. Though it give forfeiture of Life, Lands and Goods, yet no Corruption of Blood.

4. *Paine fort & dure*, in cafe of ſtanding Mute.

Burglary.

Burglary.

WE come to the Offences against the dwelling or habitation; and that of two kinds:
1. Burglary.
2. Arson, or Burning.

Burglary by the Common Law is, where a person in the Night-time breaketh and entreth into the Mansion-House of another, to the intent to commit some Felony within the same, whether the Felonious intent be executed or not.

I. What shall be said in the Night?

By some, after Sun-set and before Sun rising it is Night. *Dalt.c.*99.
But it seems, that so long as the C. PC c.14. Countenance of a person may be discerned, it is Day. *Coron.*293.

II. What

Burglary.

II. What *Breaking and Entring?*

The Entring into a Houſe by the Doors open, is a Breaking in Law but here not ſufficient without a[n] actual breaking: Therefore if the Door be open, or Window be open and the Thief draw out Goods thereby, no Burglary.

But if the Thief break the Window, draw the Latch, unlock the Door, break a Hole in the Wall, theſe are Breaking.

And as there muſt be a Breaking ſo there muſt be an Entry:

Setting the Foot over the Threſhold:

§. Putting the Hand, or a Hook or a Piſtol within the Window, o[r] Door:

Turning the Key where the Doo[r] is locked on the inſide:

§. An Entry.

In ſome caſes Burglary withou[t] actual Breaking.

Diver[s]

Burglary.

Divers come to commit Burglary, and one does it, the rest watch at the Lanes end, Burglary in all.

A Thief goes down a Chimney to rob, Burglary. _{Crom. 30.}

Thieves having an intent to rob, raise Hue and Cry, and bring the Constable, to whom the Owner opens the Door, and when they come in, they bind the Constable and rob the Owner, Burglary. _{C.PC. 14.}

A Thief assaults the House, the Owner for fear throws out his Mony, it seems not Burglary, but only Robbery.

A Thief gets in by the Doors open in the day, lies there till night, then robs and goes away, no Burglary: But if he break open the door to go out, Burglary. _{Dalt. 99.}

The Servant opens the Window to let in a Thief, who comes in and steals; Burglary in the Stranger, but Robbery in the Servant. _{Dalt. ubi supra.}

If *A.* enter into the Hall by the Doors open, the Owner retires to a Chamber, and there *A.* breaks in, this is a Breaking and Entring.

If Thieves enter into an House through a Hole made there before, no Burglary.

Trin. 16 Jac. Edmond's cafe.   *A.* lies in one part of the House, *B.* his Servant in another, between them a Stair-foot-door latched, the Servant in the night draws the Latch, and enters his Masters Chamber to Murther him, Burglary.

III. What *Mansion House?*

The Church a Mansion House within the Law.

§. The Out-buildings, as Barns Stables, are parcel of the Mansion House, and Burglary may be committed in them.

Nota, *L'use ore est, si soit u. Barne ou Stable* disjoyned at any distance from the House, *n'est Burg*lary.

Burglary may be committed in a Mansion house, though all person be out upon occasion.

So if a man hath two Houses, and sometimes live in one, sometime in another.

Burglary.

A Shop parcel of a Manſion-houſe.

A Chamber in an Inns of Court, where a perſon uſually lodges, a Manſion houſe.

But a Booth is not, and therefore remedy eſpecially provided *per Stat.* 5 *E.*6.*c.*9.

But an Indictment *quod fregit clauſum ad ipſum interficiendum*, no Felony, for no Manſion houſe.

A. leaſes to *B.* a Shop, parcel of his Houſe, to work in, where *B.* works in the day, which is broken, Ruled not Burglary, becauſe ſevered per Leaſe. *Trin.* 17 *Jac.*

IV. With *Intent* to commit ſome Felony.

If the Houſe be broken and en- C.PC. *c.* 14. red with an Intent to commit a Treſpaſs, as to beat the Owner, no Felony.

If with intent to commit a Rape, by ſome no Burglary, becauſe no Felony at Common Law; but this ſeems otherwiſe, though the Felony be not done.

Burglary.

The Indictment runs, *Burglariter & felonice domum, &c. fregerunt vel intraverunt ad ipsum, &c. interficiendum.*

And by the Stat. of 18 *El. c.* 6. Clergy taken away in all Burglary.

Arson.

Arson.

Burning is Felony at Common Law, by any that shall maliciously and voluntarily burn the House of another.

Burning.

Setting Fire on a House, without burning it, or any part of it, no Felony; but if part of the House be burnt thereby, it is Felony by Common Law.

Maliciously.

A. intending to burn only the House of *B.* thereby burns the House of *C.* this is Felony; and he may be Indicted, That *ex malitia præcogit'* he burnt the House of *C.*

A. maliciously burns his own House, to the intent to burn others, but none else but his own burnt, ruled no Felony, but a great misdemeanour; upon which set in the Pillory, and bound perpetually to Good Behaviour. 9 *Car. B. R. Haines's* Case.

Arson.

Mes si le meason d'autre p̄c̄ est combure, est Felony.

The *House*.

In-set House, or Out-set House.

If parcel of the Manſion Houſe, as Stable, Mill houſe, Sheep-houſe, Barn, and no Clergy.

§. But burning of a Barn, not parcel of a Manſion-Houſe, if it hath Corn or Hay in it, Felony, otherwiſe not.

But Felon not ouſt of Clergy, unleſs part of the Manſion Houſe or Barn with Corn.

Burning the Frame of an Houſe by 37 *H.* 8. attempting to burn a ſtack of Corn, by 3 & 4 *E.* 6. made Felony, but both Repealed 1 *Ma.*

But in *Northumberland*, *Cumberland*, *Weſtmerland*, and *Durham*, Felony to burn a ſtack of Corn by 43 *El.c.* 3.

Nota, The Indictment of Burglary, *Domum Manſionalem*; of Arſon only, *Domum*.

Breach.

Breach of Prison.

Now we come to those Felonies that are the *hindrance of amesning a Felon to publick Justice*; And they are of three kinds in reference to the person that causeth it:

1. In the party himself:
   { Breach of Prison.
   { Escape.

2. In the Officer or Person that permits it; and then,
   { Voluntary.
   { Involuntary.

3. In a Stranger, that is Rescue.

1. *Breach of Prison.*

At Common Law it seems all breach of Prison, Felony; but by Stat. 1 E. 2. *nullus de cætero, qui prisonam fregerit, subeat Judicium vitæ vel membrorum pro fractione prisonæ, nisi causa, pro qua capt' & imprisonat' fuerit, tale Judicium requirit.*

And herein thefe things are confiderable:

1. Who may *Arreſt* or Impriſon?
2. What a *Priſon*?
3. What *breaking* a Priſon?
4. What a *Cauſe* that requires a Judgment to make this Felony?

Arreſt.

Arrest.

WHo may Arrest or Imprison? This is either,
1. By a private Person.
2. By a publick Officer.
  1. Arrest *by a private Person,* and that two kinds:
      1. Either commanded and enjoyned by Law.
      2. Or permitted and allowed by Law. C.PC.f.53.

Arrest *commanded* by Law.
1. Persons present at the committing of a Felony must use their endeavours to apprehend the Offender, otherwise they are to be fined and imprisoned. St.PC.c.29.

Hence it is that if a Murther be committed in the day in a Town not inclosed, the Township shall be amerced; if in a Walled Town, be Night or Day, the Town shall be amerced [if Offender escape.] *Stat.* H.7.1.

So

So it seems if one strike anothe[r] dangerously, though death hath no[t] yet hapned.

C. P. C. 25.

2. Upon *Hue and Cry* well levie[d] every man may and must arrest th[e] Offender upon whom it is levied, b[y] *Stat. Winchester*: And want of pu[r]suit thereof is punishable by Fi[ne] and Imprisonment.

The *manner of levying Hue a[nd] Cry* is, where a Felony is committe[d] or a dangerous stroke given, res[ort] to the Constable, declare the Fa[ct] describe the party and the way [he] is gone, who thereupon is to ra[ise] the Town, be it by Night or Day, a[nd] to give the next Constable warni[ng] and he the next.

3. In aid of an Officer that h[as] a lawful Warrant *in fact*, or in L[aw] to arrest a Malefactor.

Dalt. fo. 249.

And in these cases it seems it [is] in the power of such private per[sons] to break the House, if upon dem[and] he cannot be admitted to take [the] Offender. 7 *E.* 3. 16.

Coke Jur. Courts 177.

Videtur, 1. *Sur felony fait & suspicion ascun poit arrester.* 2 *E.* 4
2.

2. *Sur Arreſt dt° ameſner al Common Gaol*, 20 E. 4. 6. *ou deliver al Conſtable*, 10 E. 4. 1.

2. A *permiſſive* Arreſt by a private perſon:

If a felony in Fact be committed, and a private perſon ſuſpect another upon a probable cauſe, he may be arreſted, though in truth innocent: And theſe may be *Probable Cauſes*;

Hue and Cry levied;
§. Company with the Offender;
§. Goods in his Cuſtody;
§. Living vagrantly;
§. Common Fame.

But upon ſuch ſuſpicion he cannot break open the Door of a Houſe, but may enter the Door being open. C.*Jur.Courts* 179.

The perſon Arreſted by either of theſe means by a private perſon, muſt be brought to the Conſtable; and if Conſtable be not to be found, Dalt. fo. 414. to a Juſtice; and in caſe of a Felony known, put in the Stocks or Common Gaol till he be brought to a Conſtable.

2. Arreſt

Arrest.

2. Arrest *by a publick Officer*, with out Process of Law.

'*Nota*, Whatsoever a private person may do in this case, an Officer as private person may do.

Now these *Officers*,
   1. *Constable*.

If complaint be made to a Constable of Felony committed, or of dangerous Blow given, though the party not dead; or in case there an assault upon the Constable, or case of any other breach of the Peace, the Constable may imprison the party in the Stocks, in the Gaol or in his House, till he can bring him before a Justice of Peace.

But if it be a bare breach of the Peace, unless it be in his view, he cannot Arrest the party; but complaint must be made to a Justice Peace: For the Constable is but Conservator, not Justice of Peace unless a Felony be done.

If a Constable see an Affray, and the Malefactors fly into another County before arrest, he may pursue

Arrest.

...e them and Arrest them there, ...nd then he must bring them before ...Justice of that County where Arrested.

But if the Escape was after Arrest, then he may retake them in ...other County, and bring them to ...e first.

He may break open Doors to *Dalt.c.78.* ...ke an Offender, where Felony ...mmitted, or a dangerous Wound ...ven.

2. By a Justice of Peace, who ...on complaint may issue out his ...arrant to apprehend the party:

1. A General Warrant to search *C.Jur.Courts* ...r Felons or stolen Goods, not *177.* ...od.

2. If a Justice hath cause of suspi...on, he may arrest as a common ...rson, not as a Justice.

3. Upon complaint of a Felony ...mmitted, and where doubt may ...e of apprehending the Offender, ...e assistance of the party suspect...g, he may grant his Warrant to ...e Constable to apprehend the ...rty, but the party suspecting
ought

ought to be present, because it is h
Arrest.

But by virtue of such Warra[nt]
Doors cannot be broken up.

4. But at the Sessions the Justic[e]
may award a *Capias* against t[he]
Person indicted, and by virt[ue]
thereof the Sheriff may break op[en]
Doors.

A party being apprehended [by]
such Warrant, is either to be Co[m]
mitted, Bailed, or Discharged.

The *Commitment* by a Justice oug[ht]
to be to the Common Gaol, by [the]
Stat. 23 *H.*8. *c.*2. and the *Mittin*[us]
ought to be,

C. M. *Car.*99.   1. Under Seal.
Stat.3 *H.*7. *c.*3.   2. Contain the Cause.
3. Have an apt Conclusion, [&]
there to stay till deliver[ed]
by Law, otherwise the W[ar]
rant void.

C.PC.c.100.
fo.209.

And Note, That a person Co[m]
mitted for Treason, Felony, [or]
other Crime, cannot be *dischar*[ged]

Arrest.

ill indicted and acquitted; or *Igno-amus* found, or discharged by Proclamation, or by the Kings Bench upon *Habeas Corpus*.

Bail.

Bail.

IN order to the consideration Arrests and Escapes, here fit consider of Bail and Mainprize cases of Felony.
1. What Bail is?
2. In what cases?
3. By whom?

1. *Bail*, are Sureties taken by Person authorized, to appear at a da and to answer and be justified l the Law.

The difference between Bail a Mainprize is, That Mainpernors a only Surety, but Bail is a Custod and therefore the Bail may resei the Prisoner if they doubt he w fly, and detain him and bring h before a Justice; and the Justi ought to commit the Prisoner discharge of the Bail; or put h to find new Sureties: The like m be done by the Justices in case insufficient Bail.

If a Juſtice of Peace take inſufficient Bail, and the party appear not, the Juſtice finable by Juſtice of Gaol Delivery.

The *ſufficiency* of the Bail in reſpect of their number, two at leaſt; and thoſe Subſidy men in caſe of Felony.

And in reſpect of the ſum, Forty Pounds at leaſt.

Bail is either in a certain ſum; or *corpus pro corpore*, in which caſe the Offender not appearing, the Surety ſhall not be Executed, but only fined. 29 *Aſſ*.44.

2. *In what Caſes?*

1. *Generally:* To refuſe Bail where the party ought to be bailed, the party offering the ſame is finable, as a Miſdemeanour:

§. And admitting Bail when it ought not, is puniſhable by the Juſtice of Gaol Delivery by Fine, or puniſhable as a negligent Eſcape at Common Law, *de quo infra*.

2. *Particularly:* At Common Law Bail in all Caſes but Homicide: But now the *Stat. Weſtm.* 1. c. 15. directs

Bail.

directs in what Cases bailable, and what not?

At this day, in all Offences below Felony, the party accused is bailable, unless

1. Ousted by that *Statute*, or some other *Statute*.
2. Unless Judgment be given.

Crom. 154.

If a Person be brought before a Justice, if it appears no Felony be committed, he may discharge him; but if a Felony be committed, though it appears not that the party accused is guilty, yet he cannot discharge him, but must commit or bail him.

The cases of Felony wherein the parties are not bailable, are

1. In *respect of the hainousness o*[f] the Offence.
   1. In a Charge of Treason against the King's Person:
   §. Counterfeiting the Seal:

Dalt. c. 114.

§. Falsifying Mony.
2. Arson, or burning Houses.
3. In a Charge of Homicide.
   1. In case of a Charge of Murther Justices of Peace cannot bail; bu[t] th[e]

the King's Bench may; but do not in difcretion, for the *Stat. Weftm.* 1. extends not to that Court. ^{Dal. c. 114. V.C fuper Stat.}

2. In cafe of Manflaughter, though it be but *Se defendendo*, and fo appear to the Juftices of Peace, they cannot bail the party accufed:

1. If he confefs the Fact upon Examination: ^{Dalt.c.114.}

2. If taken with the manner, if apparently known or manifefted that he killed another.

But if it be a *Non liquet* that he is the Perfon, and the Charge but Manflaughter, there it feems they may bail.

So if he have given a dangerous ftroke, he may be bailed till the party dead.

But fuch Bailment where Manflaughter or other Felony committed, muft be

1. By two Juftices, one of the Quorum.

2. After Examination, &c.

And thefe be all the perfons excluded from Bail fimply, in refpect of the nature of the Offence: Hence ^{3 H.7.c.9. St. 1 & 2 Ph. & Ma. c. 13.}

H 2   1. All

Bail.

C.Weſt.1.c.15.

St.PC. c. 18.

1. All Acceſſories before or after any Offence bailable; but if the Principal be attainted, and Acceſſory indicted, he ſhall not be bailed until he hath pleaded to the Indictment.

2. Perſons indicted of Larceny before the Sheriff, if of good Name.

3. Impriſonment for a light ſuſpicion, if of good Name.

4. Indicted or accuſed of petty Larceny only.

5. Appellee of Approver after death of Approver.

6. Accuſed for Treſpaſs, for which a man ought not to loſe life or member, if bail not taken away by a ſubſequent *Stat.*

Dalt c.114.
fo.304.

And hence alſo a party indicted for Burglary or Robbery may be bailed.

2. As bail is ouſted in ſome caſes, in reſpect of the greatneſs and conſequence of the Offence charged, ſo it is in *reſpect of the Notoriety* of the Offence: For bail is, when *Stat indifferenter*, whether the party be guilty or no: but when that indifferency

Bail.

ferency is removed, the Offender otherwise bailable is become not bailable.

1. If a Person be Attaint by Utlary of any Felony, yet if the Defendant comes in and pleads in avoidance of the Utlary, be it in Appeal or Indictment, the King's Bench may bail him. Westm.1. c.15

2. If he be convict by Verdict or Confession of any Felony, he is not bailable. Dalt.c.114.

But if a man be convict of Manslaughter *Se defendendo*, the Justices of *B.R.* or Gaol Delivery, or Special Writ may bail him, but not Justices of Peace: So if he have Charter of Pardon. Dalt.383.

3. He that becomes an Approver cannot be bailed.

4. He that Abjures cannot be bailed.

5. He that's taken with the manner not bailable: And consequently neither he that's taken freshly upon Hue and Cry. *Bridge*'s Case. Justice of Peace fined 40 *l.* for bailing such

Bail.

6. He that breaks Prison, not bailable.

7. Open and notorious Thieves, not bailable.

But he that is taken for a light Suspicion, bailable.

But if the Presumption be strong, or the Defamation great, the Justices may refuse to bail him: This lies in discretion.

8. Those that are Appealed by Provers; unless,
   1. The Prover die.
   2. The Prover waive his Appeal.
   3. Unless he be of good Name.

And the Reason hereof, because when the Approver appeals another, he confesseth himself guilty, and therefore induceth a presumption of guilt in another.

But this concerns not Justices of Peace, because no man can become Approver before them; because they cannot assign a Coroner; but they may take the Confession by way of Evidence.

But

But a bare Indictment or Appeal did not induce such a presumption that may hinder the bailing of a Person otherwise bailable. V. *Stat. Westm.* 1.c. 25.

But in Appeals of Death the Court in discretion admit not the Defendant to bail, but upon weighty cause. S.PC.18.

If the party be acquitted within the year upon Indictment, he is not to be discharged, but remanded or bailed at discretion, that an Appeal may be prosecuted against him. 3 *H.* 7.c. 1.

3. *Who may take* bail, or bail Offenders?

Bail was taken either *virtute brevis*, or *ex officio.*

1. Bail taken *virtute brevis*, that was either General or Special.

The General Writs.

Homine replegiando.

Habeas Corpus in the King's Bench.

Writ of Mainprise; this was directed to the Sheriff, commanding him to deliver by the Mainprise of

Bail.

Twelve, the party indicted before him.

St.PC.77.
But now by *Stat.* 28 *E.* 3. *c.* 9. these Inquests before Sheriff are taken away, and consequently the Writ of Mainprize.

Special Writ, as where a party is convict of Manslaughter *Se defendendo*; a Special Writ to certifie the ⸺

2. Bail *ex officio*.

1. The *King's Bench*, who have a higher Power than any other Power.

1. They may either in case of an Original Suit, by Indictment or Appeal before them; or upon an Indictment or Commitment returned to them, by *Habeas Corpus* or *Certiorari*, bail where another Court cannot:

In case of Murther. *B.* Mainprise, 60, 63, &c.

In the cases prohibited by *Stat. Westm.* 1. *c.* 15. V. *Cook ibid. verb. Viscounts*, & *autres verb. ne soient replevisable*.

2. *Justices of Gaol Delivery*, who may bail in cases where Justices of

Peace

Peace cannot, if it be of a thing within their cognizance.

§. As a perſon convict of Manſlaughter *Se defendendo*;

§. Or a perſon convict of Manſlaughter, that hath a Pardon to plead.

3. Juſtices of Peace.

§. 1. They cannot Bail in any caſe, but where they have cognizance of the cauſe; therefore if taken upon proceſs of Rebellion out of *Chancery* they cannot bail.

2. The *Statutes* that give power to Juſtices of Peace to bail in caſe of Felony, are 3 *H*.7.c.3. 1 & 2 *Ph. & Ma.* c. 13. upon which two kinds of Bailments.

1. Upon the firſt Accuſation, and before Examination, and that doubtleſs muſt be done,

 1. By two Juſtices, whereof one of *Quorum*.

 2. After Examination taken Cr. 156. concerning the Offence.

2. After Commitment : And though ſome Opinion be that he may be bailed by one Juſtice, yet it

ſeems

seems otherwise; for the *Stat.* (
1 *R.* 3. that gave power to one
stands repealed by 3 *H.*7.

3. After Indictment and Proce[ss]
thereupon issued in case of Trespa[ss]
or Misdemeanour, or Penal *Statute*
not prohibiting Bail, he may be baile[d]
by two Justices, whereof one of th[e]
Quorum; and by some by one Justic[e]
and thereupon may grant a *Superse*[deas]
to the *Exigent*. But it seems th[is]
holds not upon a Process upon I[n]
dictment of Felony. *Quære.*

4. The Sheriff, Baily, or Office[r]
which was of Indictment befo[re]
them: But these are removed fro[m]
that power, as it seems by the *St*[at.]
28 *E.*3.*c.*9.

1 *E.*3. 4.*c.*3. whereby they are n[ot]
to make Process, but to remove the[m]
to the Sessions of the Peace.

Rumpe

Rumper Prison.

NOW having considered the Persons that may Arrest and Bail, it makes way to consider the Offence against such Arrest or Imprisonment, by breaking such Prison,&c. And herein ensues the second Consideration.

2. What *a Prison* within this State?
  1. The Stocks.
  2. The Prison of a Lord of a Franchise.
  3. The Custody of any that Lawfully arrests, or the House of the Constable, or other person where detained.
  4. The Church, where a person abjuring is.
  5. The Prison of the Ordinary, which is now ousted, *Stat.* 23 *H.*8.*c.*11.

3. What

3. What *a breaking* ?

If the Prifon be fired without th[e] privity of the Prifoner, he may law[fully] fully break it to fave himfelf.

2. If a Gaoler do voluntari[ly] permit him to efcape, Felony in th[e] Gaoler, not in the Prifoner; but negligent, Felony in the Prifoner, a[nd] Mifdemeanour in the Gaoler.

3. If Prifoner under Cuftody [be] refcued, or Prifon broke by Strange[rs] without his procurement, no Felon[y] in the Prifoner.

4. Going out the Doors open, n[o] Felony; for the *Statute* requires a[n] actual breaking.

4. *Nifi caufa* ; *tale judicium,&c.*

1. If *A*. mortally wound *B*. an[d] is committed, and he break Prifo[n] and *B*. then die, no Felony.

2. If a Felony made by a fubf[e]quent *Statute*, and an Offend[er] committed therefore, break Prifo[n] Felony.

3. Con

3. Committed for suspicion of [fe]lony, yet if a Felony done, breaking [P]rison Felony.

4. If the Offence for which the [pa]rty was committed appear not by [M]atter of Record, necessary a Felony [be] done, else breach of Prison no [Fe]lony.

But if it appear by Matter of Re[co]rd, and the party taken by *Capias*, [if] he break Prison, Felony, though no [Fe]lony done.

5. If Felony was done, yet breach [of] Prison no Felony, unless a lawful [M]*ittimus, de quo suprà*.

6. The Indictment for the breach [mu]st be Special, that it may appear [he] was committed for Felony.

5. *Tale Judicium requirit*.

1. Breach of Prison turns into [Fe]lony only, though the party were [co]mmitted for Treason.

But if a Prisoner break a Prison [w]herein Traytors are, to let out the [T]raytors, this is Treason.

2. A man imprisoned for Pet Larceny, or *Se defendendo*, break Prison, no Felony.

3. If a Prisoner break Prison, h may be Arraigned of that before be convict of the first Felony.

V.Dalt.331. But a Gaoler permitting a volu tary Escape shall not be Arraigned t the Prisoner be first Attaint; for the Prisoner be acquit, the Esca dispunishable.

Escap

Escape in the Party.

N*Ota*, If a Perſon eſcapes before Arreſt, not puniſhable in him Felony; but for the Flight, he rfeits Goods when preſented.

In caſe a man ſlain in the day, if e Offender Eſcape, Townſhip nerced. *Vide ſupra.*

Iſſint ſi ſoit dangerouſment Wound, H 7. c. 1. *Et ſi ſoit vill immure ſer' nerce, ſoit ceo in jour ou nuit,* 3 E. 3. oron. 299. Stat. Winton, cap. 4.

Eſcape.

Escape in the Officer, or him that makes Arrest.

This is either in case of Arrest
1. By a Stranger.
2. By an Officer.

If *a Stranger* Arrest a man fc Felony, or suspicion thereof, an deliver him over to four others, an they receive him and let him go a large, this is an Escape in both; fc the first man should have delivere him to the Constable; and the latte should not have let him go at larg(

And the same Law seems to b for an Escape by a Stranger tha hath a Prisoner in his Custody, a for an Officer in case of Escap voluntary or negligent.

Escape by an Officer.

Escape of an Officer.
1. *Negligent.*
   1. Bailing a person not bailable, through ignorance, by one that hath power to bail; a negligent Escape.

   But it seems if done by a Gaoler a voluntary Escape; because he hath no such power.

   2. The ordinary punishment of a Negligent Escape.
      1. Of a party Attaint, 100 *l.*
      2. Of a party Indict, 5 *l.*
      3. Of a party not Indict, at discretion.

   3. For Insufficiency of the Gaoler, the Sheriff must answer for Negligent Escapes.

4. A Gaoler *de facto*, though not *de jure*, muſt anſwer for Eſcapes.

5. If after a negligent Eſcape the Gaoler retake him upon freſh Suit before he be puniſhed, it excuſeth.

If the Conſtable bring a perſon to Gaol, the Gaoler refuſeth him, the Vill ſha[ll] be charged, and Gaole[r] fined.

2. *Voluntary* Eſape.

St. 14 E. 3. c. 10.

1. Hath the ſame Crime that th[e] perſon permitted to Eſcape ſtoo[d] committed for, *viz.* Treaſon or F[e]lony.

2. But this is in the immediat[e] perſon that permits it; and ther[e]fore though civilly the Sheriff mu[ſt] anſwer for Offences of Gaoler, y[et] not criminally.

3. There muſt be a Felony reall[y] done, and a Commitment by a law[]ful Warrant.

4. If within the year the Priſon[er] be acquitted upon Indictment, yet voluntary Eſcape is puniſhable [as]
Fel[ony

Felony, because Wife intituled to her Appeal.

5. The Escape if voluntary, punishable *ut supra*, though the Prisoner were not indicted. ^{Dalt. fo.335. Dyer 99.}

I 2 *Rescue.*

Rescue.

1. A Hindrance [of a person t[o]
be arrested that has com[mitted]
Felony is a Misdemeanor, bu[t]
no Felony.

2. But if the party be arreste[d]
and then rescued, if the arrest w[as]
for Felony, the Rescuer is a Felor[;]
if for Treason, a Traytor; becau[se]
they are all Principals.

But he shall not be arraigned t[ill]
the Principal attainted; and if t[he]
Principal die before attainder, t[he]
Rescuer shall be fined and impriso[n]ed.

3. There must be a Felony real[ly]
done, and a lawful Commitment.

N. *Rescue hors de custody de C[on]stable, &c. est Felony, licet ne f[uit]
amesne al Gaol.*

Feloni[ous]

Felonies by the Statute. C.Pl.C.c.4.

3. **H***En.7.cap.14.*
Imagining and *conspiring* to kill the King, or any of his Council.
§. Clergy not taken away.
1 *Jac.c.*12.
§. *Witchcraft, de quo supra.*
§. 25 *H.* 8. *c.* 6. Revived by 5 *El. c.*17.
Buggery with Man or Beast.
§. Without benefit of Clergy.
Debet esse Penetratio, as well as *Emissio.*
In this and Rape *carnaliter cognovit.*

13 *E.* 1.*c.*34.
Rape: This was Felony at Common Law; then by *Stat. Westm.* 1. *c.* 13. made but a Misdemeanour; then by this *Statute* restored to Felony again.

And hence it is that it is not inquirable in a Leet, because though no Felony; yet it lost its nature by *W.* 1.*c.*13.   C. *fur ceo Stat.*

Felonies by the Stat.

Nul Appeal done al party.
18 *E*. 3. *Coron*. 169.
If the Woman be under ten years then though she consent, yet by *Stat*. 18 *El.c*.6. it is a Rape; if above ten years, if she consent not, a Rape though she consent after.

But in such case of a subsequent consent, the *Stat*. 6 *R*.2.*c*.6. gives the Appeal to the Husband, if none to the Father, &c.

Clergy taken away by *Stat*. 18 *El* *c*.7. upon Conviction by Verdict, o Confession, or Utlawed.

Cestuy que aid in Rape est Ravistor 11 *H*.4.13.

3. *H*. 7. *c*. 2.
Taking a Woman against her Wi and marrying her, Felony.

1. Such Maid, Widow, or Wif Must have Lands, Tenements, o Goods, or be Heir Apparent.

2. She must be taken against he Will.

3. She must be married or de filed.

4. Extends not to taking a War or Bondwoman.

Nota

Felonies by the Stat.

Nota, The taking away in one County, and marrying in another, indicted where married; and they may enquire of the forcible taking. 2. Privy to the Marriage, but not to the Force, not Guilty. 3. Marriage with Consent not excusing so long as she is under the Force, 13 *Car*. *Fulwood*'s Case.

All Accessories before or after, made Principals by this Act.

Clergy taken away by *Stat.* 39 *El. c.* 2.

5 *H.*4. *c.*5.

Malicious cutting out Tongue, or putting out Eyes, Felony.

Clergy not taken away.

Extends not to cutting off Ears.

8 *H.*6. *c.* 12.

Stealing, carrying away or avoiding Records, Felony. And

The Judges of either Bench enabled to hear and determine the same.

Accessories before made Principals.

§. Clergy allowable.

5 *H.*4. *c.*4.

Felonies by the Stat.

Multiplication of Gold or Silver, Felony.
 1. *H*.7.*c*.1.

Hunting unlawfully in Forests, Chases, or Warrens with painted Faces by Night, and Rescuers, *viz.* other than the party arrested, Felony.
 31 *El. c.* 4.

Imbezelling the King's Armour, &c. Felony.
  Qualifications:
   1. Ought to be impeached within a year.
   2. Offender loseth Lands but during life.
   3. No Corruption of Blood.
   4. Wife loseth not Dower.
   5. Defendant admitted to proof.
 3 *Jac.c.*4

Subjects passing Sea to serve foreign Prince, not having taken Oath of Obedience:
 No Corruption of Blood:
 Offender may have Clergy.

Articuli.

Articuli super Chartas, c. 2.

Purveyors Felons in certain Cases:
§. They may have Clergy.
39 *El. c.* 17.
Wandring Souldiers, Felons in certain cases.
§. Excluded of Clergy.
18 *H* 6.*c.*19.
Souldiers retained, as is prescribed in the Act, departing from their Captains without licenfe.
§. 2 *E.*6.*c.*2. *ad idem.*
§. Clergy excluded.
1 *Jac.* 12.
Marrying a second Husband or Wife, the former living, Felony: except Cases following;
1. The Man under fourteen, or the Wife under twelve at time of first Marriage, and not agreeing after first Espousals, may marry a second Husband or Wife.
2. A Man or Wife absent above seven years, second Marriage no Felony: If beyond Sea, though notice
of

Felonies by the Stat.

1 Jac.11. of life: If in *England*, then withou notice.

3. After a Divorce, though *à menſ & thoro* only.

4. After a Nullity declared of th former Marriage by Ecclesiastic Court,

    Offenders have Clerg

1 *Jac.c.* 31.

§. For going with a Plague Soi but this discontinued.

14 *El.* 3. 20.

Gaoler compelling Prisoner Dures to become Appellor, Felor whether the Appellees be acquitt or not.

3 *H.* 5. *c.* 1.

Coining, or bringing in Ga half pence, Suskins, or Dodkins.

§. And 2 *H.* 6. *c.* 9. payment Blanks,

    Offender hath Cler

17 *E.* 3. *n.* 15.

Transportation of Silver, or I portation of false Mony, made lony,

    Offender hath Cler

18 *H.* 6. *c.* 15.

      Exp

Felonies by the Stat.

Exportation of Wool or Woolfells, other than to the Staple of Calais.

37 E.3. 19.

Stealing Falcons, &c. or concealing the same after Proclamation, Felony.

§. Offender hath Clergy.

3 H.6. c.1.

Congreation of Masons to prevent *Statutes* of Labourers:

§. But this Obsolete by the *Statute* 5 *El.* the Acts to which it relates are repealed.

27 El. c. 2.

Receiving, retaining, or maintaining Jesuit or Popish Priest knowingly,

§. Clergy excluded.

35 El. c. 1.

Felony refusing to make Abjuration, or after Abjuration not to depart, in some case,

§. Clergy excluded.

1 & 2 Ph. & M. c. 4.

Egyptians above fourteen years, remaining here a Month.

§. And 5 *El. c.* 20. takes away Clergy.

39 El.

39 El. c 4. 1 Jac. c. 7. 25.
Dangerous Rogue adjudged to the Gallies; and returning without licenfe, Felony:
§. But Offender hath Clergy.
§. But branded Rogue, Felon, and no Clergy.

5 El. c. 14.
Forging a Deed after a form[er] Conviction.

C.PC. f. 172. If a man be convict or condemn[ed] of publifhing a forged Deed, a[nd] after he forge a Deed, this is Fel[o]ny.

If the Offence were after a form[er] but before Conviction thereof, [no] Felony.

      Clergy oufte[d]

8 El. c. 3.
Sending Sheep beyond Sea afte[r] former Conviction.

      Clergy allowe[d]

33 H. 6. c. 1.
Servants after deceafe of the Mafter, riotoufly fpoiling Goo[ds], &c.

    Offenders fhall have Cler[gy]

Felonies by the Stat.

21 *H.* 8. 7.
Servants imbezelling Goods of their Masters delivered to them, Felony;
But the *Statute* of 27 *H*.8. *c.* 17. that took away Clergy, being Repealed by 1 *E*.6.*c.* 12. they may now have Clergy.
22 *H.* 8. *c.* 11. 2 & 3 *Ph.* & *Ma.* 19.
Cutting Powdike, Felony,
   Offender hath Clergy.
43 *El.c.* 13.
Detaining persons in *Cumberland*, &c. against their Will, and giving or receiving Blackmail, &c. Felony,
   Without Clergy.

Mispri-

Misprisions.

NOW we come to Offenc[es] Criminal, but *not* Capita[l] and thofe of two kinds:
1. Offences by Common Law:
2. Offences againſt ſpecial St[a]tutes.

Offences by *Common Law* n[ot] Capital, are either greater Offenc[es] or leſſer:

Greater; and thoſe come und[er the] name of *Miſpriſions*, which again a[re] of two ſorts:

Negative, in not doing that th[ey] ought, or of Omiſſion.

Poſitive, in doing ſome great M[iſ]demeanour they ought not.

Miſpriſio[n]

Misprision of Treason.

The Negative *Misprisions.*

Misprision *of Treason.* All Treason includes Misprision: The Concealing of any Treason, is declared Misprision only by the *Statute* of 1 & 2 *Mar.c.*10. *que iduce auxi misprision.* 2 R. 3. 9. C.PC.c.3.
But this in case of bare knowledge; for if knowledge and Assent, is Treason: and though the Treason be by *Statute*, yet the concealing thereof is Misprision of Treason.
Every man therefore that knoweth Treason, must with all speed reveal to the King, his privy Council, or other Magistrate.
He that receives and comforts a Traytor knowingly, be it a Counterfeiter of Coin or other, is a Principal Traytor, and not only guilty of Misprision. *Abingdon*'s Case against the Opinion in *Dyer* 296. *Conier*'s Case. C.PC.c.64.

The

Misprision of Treason.

The *Judgment* in case of Misp[ri]sion of Treason is Imprisonme[nt] during life, forfeiture of Goods, fo[r]feiture of profits of Land duri[ng] life.

Nota, *Si un conust un que ad cou[nter]terfeit Coigne, & ne luy discover, Misprision de Treason. Mes si solement utter counterfeit coigne scia[nt] ceo estre counterfeit n'est Mispris[ion] de Treason, mes serra Fine & I[m]prison. Issint resolve a* Newg[ate] 1661.

Misprision of Felony.

2. **M**isprision *of Felony*, is either by Common Law, or by *Statute*.

By the Common Law a concealment of a Felony, or procuring of the concealing thereof.

The Punishment.

1. If a common Person, Fine and Imprisonment.
2. If an Officer, as Sheriff, Coroner, Imprisonment for a year, and Ransom at the King's pleasure, by *Stat. W. 1. c. 9.*

By the *Stat.* 3 *H.*7.*c.*1. 33 *H.*8.*c.*6. the knowing of an unlawful Assembly, and not discovering it within 24 hours.

Concealment of Jurors, *vide Stat.*

Theftbote.

3. **T***Heftbote*, which is more than a bare Misprision o Felony, and is where the Owne doth not know the Felony, bu takes his Goods again, or other A mends, not to Prosecute.

But taking the Goods again bare ly, no offence, unless he favour th Thief.

The punishment hereof is Ran som and Imprisonment.

Misprision

Misprisions Positive, *or of Commission.*

1. **D**Iscovery by one of the Grand Inquest of the persons Indicted, or Evidence against them, Misprision, punishable by Fine and Imprisonment, but no Felony, nor Treason.   *C. PC. c.46.*

2. A person dissuading Witnesses from bringing in Evidence against a Felon is no Accessory, but a great Misprision, punishable by Fine and Imprisonment.   *C. PC. c.64.*

3. Reproaching a Judge, assaulting an Attorney against him, or abusing a Juror that gave verdict against him; a great Misprision, punishable by Fine and Imprisonment.

4. Rescuing a Prisoner from the Bar of the Courts of *B. R. Canc. B. C.* or *Exchequer*, a Misprision for which the party shall lose his Hand, Goods, Profits of Lands, during Life, and perpetual Imprisonment.

5. If a man strike sitting the four Courts at *Westminster*, in the pre-

Misprisions Positive.

fence of the Court, the like Judgment

6. If in presence of those Courts, or before Justices of Assize or *Oyer & Terminer*, a person draw his Sword upon any Judge or Justice, though he strikes not, or strike another, like Judgment.

7. By *Stat.* 33 *H.*8.*c.*12. striking in the King's presence, drawing blood; loss of Hand and perpetual Imprisonment, Fine and Ransom.

8. By *Stat.* 14 *El. c.*3. forging of Money not current, Misprision of Treason.

9. Stranger uttering false Money made within this Realm, knowing it Counterfeit, 3 *H.*7.10.

10. A Lord of Parliament, departing from Parliament, 3 *E.*3.

Maihem.

Maihem.

ANd hither we may refer *Maihem*, which though it be a particular Crime, for which Appeal lieth, yet it is not Felony of death.

Cutting off the Hand, or striking out a Tooth, Maihem; but not cutting off the Ear. ^{C. CP. c. 40.}

The Judgment is only Fine and Damages; and therefore if recovery in Trespass, it is a good bar in Appeal of Maihem.

Offences not Capital.

Ffences of an Inferiour nature:
They are either such as are committed by an Officer:
  Neglect of Duty,
  Bribery,
  Extortion.
Or such as refer to a common person, without relation to Office, and those reducible to three kinds:

1. Breaches of publick Peace, and therein,
   1. Of Affrays.
   2. Of Riots.
   3. Of Forcible Entries.
   4. Barretries.
   5. Riding armed.
2. Deceipts and Cozenage.
3. Nusances.

   Decay of Bridges.
   Decay of High-ways.
   Inns and Alehouses.

Breach of the Peace.

AFFRAY, If Weapons drawn, or ftroke given or offered; but Words no Affray: Menace to kill or beat, no Affray; but yet for fafeguard of Peace, Conftable may bring them before Juftice.

In Affrays confiderable,
1. What a *private Man* may do?
Private perfons may ftay Affray⸗ers till heat over, and deliver them to Conftable.

If perfon hurt another dange⸗ roufly, private perfon may arreft the Offender, and bring him to Gaol or next next Juftice. Dalt. c.8.

2. What by a *Conftable*?
    1. Affray in prefence of a Conftable, he ought to do his endeavour to fupprefs it, otherwife finable.
    2. If an Affrayer fly to a houfe, or if made in a houfe, Con⸗ftable

Breach of the Peace.

stable may break open house to preserve Peace, or take the Offender.

3. If in Affray Assault be made upon the Constable, he may strike again, or imprison Offender.

4. Constable may in such case imprison, till he find Surety of Peace.

5. But it seems if Affray past, and not in view of Constable, he cannot imprison without Warrant of the Justice, unless Felony done, or like to be done.

3. What by a *Justice* ?

1. In his presence, the same Power that a private person or Constable, and may imprison till Surety of Peace found; the like upon Complaint.

2. If dangerous hurt, Justice may imprison till appear whether the party die or live, or bail the party.

The former better discretion.

Riot.

Breach of the Peace. 137

Riot.

When above the number of Two ...eet to do some unlawful act, and ...) act it; but if they meet and act ... not, an unlawful Assembly, in ...wer of Justices to suppress them, ... *H*.4. *c*.7.

A man for safeguard of his house ...ainst Malefactors or Trespassers, ...y assemble his Friends for his ...:fence.

But he cannot assemble to pre-...nt a beating threatned in his pre-...ice.

Riot recorded by one Justice upon ...:w traversable; by two, not, be-...ise pursuant to the *Statute*.

Forcible

Forcible Entry.

Forcible Entry muſt be either
Manu forti,
Furniſhed with unuſual Weapo[ns]
Menace of life or limb.
Breaking open door:
Contra, it ſeems, if door o[nly]
latched,
Ejecting forcibly the poſſeſſors
Cum multitudine gentium, one m[ay]
commit a Force, three at leaſ[t a]
Riot.

Forc[

Forcible Detainer.

Menacing the Poffeffor to go out on pein of lofs of life or limb.
Unufual Weapons or Company.
§. Refufing to admit the Juftice to me in to view the Force.
Detainer with Force juftifiable, ere party in poffeffion Three rs:
§. But though his Poffeffion law-, yet if within the Three years ually removed, though reftored the Juftices, enables not a De-er with Force.
But if the Three years Poffeffion h been by Force, then the laft cible Detainer punifhable, and ders not Reftitution.
f a Diffeifee within the Three rs make lawful Claim, this an rruption of his Poffeffion.

Reftitution.

Reſtitution.

1. *By whom?*
 1. Juſtices *B. R.* may reſt upon Indictment removed bef[ore] them.
 2. One Juſtice of Peace can[not] reſtore upon an Indictment be[fore] them; nor Seſſions of Peace, un[less] upon Indictment found at S[eſſi]ons.
 3. It ſeems Juſtices of Gaol [De]very or *Oyer* and *Terminer*, car[not] Reſtore.

2. *How?*
Upon View.
Upon Indictment?
 Muſt be ſufficient,
  Adhuc extra tenet.
If Erroneous, may be ſuperſ[eded] by the ſame Juſtice before Execu[tion.] After it is Executed, then Re-reſ[titu]tion in *B. R.* upon Indictment qu[aſh]ed.

Restitution *stayed*.
   By *Certiorari*.
   By quashing Indictment.
   By pleading thereunto, which
     is nevertheless in discretion.

Barretry.

Barretry.

Riding Armed.

Going Armed.

Vid. *Stat.* 20 *R.*2.*c.*1. 7 *R.*2.*c.*1
2 *E.*2.*c.*3. *Stat.Northampton.*

Nusance

Nuſances.

3 *Ridges Publick.*
Are not chargeable upon a rticular Perſon, but *Ratione terræ.*
But of Common Right, repairable the whole County.
The manner of Repairing directed *Stat.*22 *H.*8,*c.*5.

High-

High-ways.

High-ways: Provisions,
1. For their *Enlarging* an[d]
removing Trees within 200 Foot [of]
either side.
  13 *E*. 1. *c*.5.
  5 *El*. *c*. 15.
 2. For their Amending *vide* t[he]
Stat.
  5 *El*. *c*. 13.
  29 *El*. *c*.5.
  2 & 3 *P. M. c*.8.

The *Charge* of Repair of Hig[h]
ways lies of common right upon th[e]
Parish wherein they are, unless,
 1. A Special Prescription cast
upon another.
 2. Unless the Owner of the Lan[d]
in which they are, inclose it, then
must be cast upon the Owner.

But they that have Ditches on [ei]ther side ought to scour them, 8 [&]
7. 5.

High-ways.

Inns.
Ale-houses.
Bawdy-houses.
Gaming-houses.

L   *Common*

Common Inns.

1. **A**Ny person may erect Common Inn, so it be no *ad nocumentum*.
   1. In respect of their multitud[e] when there are enough a[n]cient Inns before.
   2. In respect of the inconv[e]nience of the place or situation.
   3. In respect of Disorders the[re] permitted.
      All which are Commo[n] Nusances, and may b[e] presented and fined.

2. He that erects a Common In[n] and *refuses to entertain* Guests, ma[y] be Indicted and fined for the same.

3. If a Common Inn, contrary t[o] *Statute*, suffer persons to tipple the[re] as Ale houses, he may be compelle[d] to be bound, or may be suppresse[d] as Ale houses, or may be indicted [at] Sessions.

Al[e

Ale-houses.

SEe for *Ale-houses*, the suppressing of them, and the punishing of Tipling in them, 5 *E.* 6. *c.* 25. 1 *Jac. c.* 9. 4 *Jac. c.* 5. 7 *Jac. c.* 10. 21 *Jac. c.* 7. 1 *Car. c.* 4. 3 *Car. c.* 3.

An Ale-house-keeper suppressed, according to the *Stat.* of 5 *El.*6.*c.*25. by two Justices, whereof one of the *Quorum*, cannot be allowed but in open Sessions.

An Ale-house-keeper suppressed for the Offences 7 *Jac. c.*18. 21 *Jac. c.* 7. for suffering Tipling, or 7 *Jac. c.* 10. for selling less than is there directed, or 21 *Jac. c.* 7. for continuing drinking in another Ale-house, or 21 *Jac.* for being drunk, cannot be licensed in three years, and if he be, such License void.

5 & 6 *E.*6. *c.*25.

None to sell Ale, &c. unless licensed in open Sessions, or by two Justices, one of the *Quorum*.

Ale-houses.

Persons licensed to be bound by Recog. not to keep unlawful Games, and for using good Order.

Recog. return next Quarter Sessions.

Process upon Recognizance at Sessions.

Persons unlicensed keeping Ale-house imprisoned by two Justices, one of the *Quorum*, for three days, and till Recogn. given not to sell Ale.

Certificate of such Recogn. Conviction, and Fine 20 *s*.

1 *Jac. c* 9.

Ale men, Inn-keeper or Victualer *suffering* Inhabitant to sit *tippling*, forfeit 10 *s*. to the Poor.

Conviction before one Justice, &c. by two Witnesses.

Penalties levied by Constables, and Churchwardens by distress and sale within six days.

In default of distress. Offender committed till payment *per* Justice.

Constable, &c. neglecting to levy or certifie default of distress, forfeits 40 *s*.

4 *Jac.*

Ale-houses.

4 Jac. c. 5.

Person drunk forfeits 5 *s.* to be paid within a Week after Conviction, to the Poor: If neglect, levy by Distress, by Warrant from Justice: If not able to pay, commit to Stocks for six hours.

Constable neglecting duty, forfeits 10 *s.* to the use of the Poor.

Any person *sitting tippling*, dwelling in the same Parish, forf. 3 *s.* 4 *d.* to Poor, proved before Justice, levy *per* distress, and for want of distress commit *per* Justice to House of Correction.

Second Offence, bound to good Behaviour.

Constables, &c. bound by Oaths to present Offences.

Punishment within six Months.

21 Jac. c. 7.

Former act extend to Foreigners, as well as Inhabitants.

One Witness suffice to convict, or view of Justice.

Ale-house suppress, not licensed for three years, *per Stat. 7 Jac. c.* 10.

Ale-houses.

1 *Car.* cap. 4. Former *Statute* extend to Inn keepers and Taverns.

Offences

Offences not Capital by Statute.

Offences not Capital more particularly *by Statute*.

Forgery by *Stat.* 5 *El.* c.14.

Perjury, and Subornation thereof, 5 *El.c.*9.

Champerty, Embracery and Maintenance, 32 *H.*8.*c.*9.

Ingroffing, *Foreftalling*, and *Regrating*, 5 E.6.c.14.

Salt Victual within *Statute*.

Apples and Cherries, &c. no Victual.

Mault seems not, but Corn and Grain exprefly Victual by 5 *Ed*.6.

A Stranger, or Subject, bringing Victual into the Realm, may sell them in grofs, but the Vendee cannot; neither may any Merchant buy within the Realm, and sell in grofs.

Attempting to inhance the price of Merchandize, a kind of Foreftalling.

Selling Corn in the Sheaf, unlawful.

Matters

Matters of Religion.

Reviling the Sacraments, Imprisonment, Fine and Ran[som], 1 *E.6. c.* 1. *Repealed*, 1 *Ma.c,*2. [re]vived 1 *El.c.*7.

2. Not coming to Church to hear [co]mmon Prayer, by 5 *E. 6. c.*1. sub[jec]t to Church Censures.

Nota 3 *E. 6. c.* 1. setled a Book of [Co]mmon *Prayer*; Injoyned the use: [re]fusing to use it, using other, or [de]praving it, Imprisonment for six [m]onths for first Offence, twelve [m]onths for second, during life for [thi]rd.

5 *E. 6. c.* 1. Alters the Prayers; [bu]t applies the Penalty to the new [Bo]ok.

Nota, Repeal 1 *Ma.* that *Repealed* *Jac.c.*25.

1 *El. c.* 2. Enacts the use of the [Bo]ok of 5 *E.*6. with some Alterations. Any that,

    1. Refuse to use it:
    2. Use another form:
                  3. Deprave

Matters of Religion.

3. Deprave it.

§. If Spiritual, six Months Impr[i]sonment first Offence, one yea[r] Imprisonment second Offence, Depr[i]vation third Offence.

If Lay, first Offence 12 Mont[hs] Imprisonment, second Offence duri[ng] life.

Depraving Book of Comm[on] Prayer, first Offence 100 Mark[s] second Offence 400 Marks, thi[rd] Offence forfeit Goods and Imprisc[n]ment during life.

8 *El. c.* 1. touching Consecrati[on of] B[i]shops.

Concerning repair to Church.

1 *El.* 2. Every Sunday and Ho[ly] day, *sub pœna* 12 d. *per diem.*

§. 23 *El. c.* 1. 20 l. *per mens[em]* for absenting; and if absent twe[lve] Months upon Certificate, bound [to] good Behaviour.

29 *El. c.* 2. Conviction of Re[cu]sancy.

35 *El. c.* 1. Penalty of dissuadi[ng] from Church, holding of Conv[en]ticles, commit to Prison witho[ut] bail until Conformity.

N[o]

Matters of Religion. 155

Nonconformity within three [m]onths after Conviction, shall ab[jur]e the Realm.

Not departing, or returning, Fe[lon]y without benefit of Clergy.

Submitting, discharged of the Pe[nal]ty by this Act.

Relapsing loseth the benefit of [his] Submission.

Ten pounds *per mensem* for every [Pers]on retaining or relieving Recusant [aft]er Notice.

[C]*ap.* 2. Recusants not to remove [5] Miles from dwelling.

[1] *Jac. c.* 4. Conformable Heir of [R]ecusant discharged: Third part [disc]harged of forfeiture.

[P]enalty of sending Children to [Sem]inaries.

[3] *Jac. c.* 4 & 5. Penalty for refusing [Oa]th of Supremacy.

    1 *El. c.* 1.
    5 *El. c.* 1.
      Of Obedience,
    3 *Jac. c.* 4.
    7 *Jac. c.* 6.

King's Bench.

Now we come to confider the *Proceeding* againſt a par[ty] for Felony, and therein,
1. Concerning the *Juriſdiction* [of the] *Court* wherein Proceedings are to [be] had in Capital Cauſes; and th[ese] are principally,
   1. The King's Bench.
   2. Juſtices of Gaol Delivery.
   3. Juſtices of Oyer and T[er-]miner and Aſſizes.
   4. The Sheriff and Coroner.
   5. The Lord Steward of [the] Houſhold.

The *King's Bench*, the Supre[me] Court of Criminal Juriſdiction. is a Court of Oyer and Termi[ner,] Gaol Delivery, and Eyre, in [the] County where it ſits.

9 Rep. *San-*
thar's Caſe.

By the coming of the King's Be[nch] into any County, during the ſit[ting] thereof in that County, all po[wer] and proceedings of Commiſſio[ns] of Oyer and Terminer is ſuſpen[ded]

But a Special Commission of Oyer ᵍ·ᴾᶜ· p.27. ⟨an⟩d Terminer bearing *Teste* in the ⟨T⟩erm may be granted; and King's ⟨Be⟩nch may adjourn, and then they ⟨m⟩ay sit.

Where the King's Bench proceeds ⟨up⟩on an Offence committed in the ⟨sa⟩me County, there need not fifteen ⟨da⟩ys between the *Teste* and Return ⟨of⟩ the *Venire facias*: But if they ⟨pr⟩oceed upon a Cause removed by ⟨Ce⟩rtorari, they must have fifteen ⟨da⟩ys. 9 Rep. San-*char*'s Case.

Gaol

Gaol Delivery.

C. Jur. Courts sub hoc titulo.

1. THe Juſtices of Peace oug to deliver the Indictmen not determined unto thoſe Judg and they may Arraign any perſon Priſon upon them.

2. They may take Indictme againſt any perſon in Priſon, and may Juſtices of Oyer and Termin and herein they have a concurr Juriſdiction.

3. They may take a Pannel turned by the Sheriff without Precept.

4. They may deliver by Proc mation perſons ſuſpected, where th is no Evidence to indict them.

5. May award Execution of p ſons in Priſon utlawed before Juſti of Peace,

6. May aſſign Coroner to an A peal, and make Proceſs againſt Appellee in a Foreign County.

7. May puniſh thoſe that und bail Priſoners, *Stat. de Finibus,* 1 2 *Ph. & Ma.* c.13.

8. M

8. May deliver the Gaol of persons committed for High Treason.

9. May receive Appeals by Bill against persons in Prison.

10. By *Stat.* 9 *E.* 3. 15. must send their Records into the Treasury of the Exchequer at *Michaelmas.*

11. Others may be added to the former Commission by Commission of Association, or their power committed to fewer by *Si non omnes.*

12. By *Stat.* 2 & 3 *Ph. & Ma.* 18. a General Commission of Gaol delivery through the County determines not a Special Commission granted in a Corporation, &c. parcel thereof.

13. By *Stat.* 1 *E.* 6. *c.* 7. the subsequent Commissioners of Gaol delivery, power to give Judgment upon such as were Reprieved before Judgment by former Commissioners and Process before any former Commissioners of Peace, Gaol Delivery, Oyer and Terminer, or others not discontinued by granting new Commissions.

If a Prisoner be bailed, he is yet
in

Gaol Delivery.

in Prison to be Arraigned befor these Justices, for he is a Prisoner contrary in case of Mainprize, 21 E. 7. 33. 9 E. 4. 2. 39 H. 6. 27.

Cr. Jur. 226.   Although their Commission determine with their Session, after they are gone, they may command a Reprieve or Execution, *Dyer* 205.

Licet soit ad Gaolum deliberandu hac vice uncore pnt' adjourner lo Commission. Cr. Jur. 226.

Commission d'Oyer & Terminer, Gaol Delivery, pnt' Estoyer ensemb Ibid. Bro. Commission 24.

Justices de Gaol Delivery & Oy & Terminer, pnt' enquire per ami deux powers, and make up their Records accordingly, 9 H. 7. 9. Cr. J 226.

Oy

Oyer and Terminer.

1. The Justices Authority must be by Commission, and not by Writ, otherwise their Proceedings void. 42 *Ass.* 12.

2. They cannot proceed but upon an Indictment taken before themselves.

3. By good Opinion they may proceed the same Day or Session against a party Indicted before them. *Nota le contrar' ad estre adjudge.*

4. Where Offences are limited to be heard and determined in any Court of Record, generally it may be heard and determined by them. *Quære,* for *Gregory*'s Case *contra. Vid. Dyer* 236.

5. Others may be added, or their Power contracted by Association, or *si non omnes,* as before.

6. One sitting without Adjournment determines their Commission.

7. Juſtices of Oyer and Terminer or of Peace, cannot aſſign a Coroner, as Juſtices of Gaol Delivery may.

8. By *Stat.* 9 *E.* 3. they are alſo to ſend their Records determined into the *Exchequer.*

V.12 Aſſ.21.
9. A *Superſedeas* ſuſpends their power, and a *Procedendo* revives it but a new Commiſſion determines it; the like of Commiſſion of *Niſi prius,&c.* but it determines not without Notice.

    1. By ſhewing the new Commiſſion.

V.2 & 3 P. &
M.c.10.
    2. Or proclaiming it in the County.

    3. Or Seſſions held by new Commiſſion.

10. An Award upon the Roll not ſufficient to return a Jury, but a Precept under Seal of the Commiſſioners.

11. And *Nota,* That a Special Commiſſion of Oyer and Terminer may be granted to ſit in one County to hear and determine Treaſons, &c in another, but then the Indictment muſt

Oyer and Terminer.

must be found in proper County, and the Trial by Jurors of proper County. *C.PC.fo.27.*

M 2 *Justices*

Justices of Assize.

BY *Stat.* 27 *E.* 1. *c.* 3. *de finibus* Justices of Assize have power to deliver Gaols of Felons and Murtherers.

And by some Opinion they may do it *virtute Officii*, without any Special Commission. *S.PG.c.* 5.

But in case of Counterfeiting Coin,&c. upon *Stat.* 3 *H.*5. *Stat.*2. *c.* 7. they must have a Special Commission.

Justices of Peace.

THe *Statute* of 18 *E.* 3. *c.* 2. gives them power by Commission to hear and determine Felonies and Trespasses against the Peace.

But then there must be a special S.PC.L.2,c.5. Clause in their Commission, *Necnon ad aud' & terminand' felonias, &c.* Otherwise they cannot do it.

Yet that Clause doth not in propriety make the Justices of Peace Justices of Oyer and Terminer, because that it is a distinct Commission; and therefore a *Statute*, as that of 5 *El. c.* 14. limiting Forgery to V.C.PC.c.14. be heard and determined before Ju- Da.L.c.20. stices of Oyer and Terminer, gives 9 Rep. 118. not the power therein to Justices of Peace; but the Justices of the King's Bench are Justices of Oyer and Terminer within this *Statute*.

By force of the general words of their Commission, they may en- Dy. 67. quire of Murther at their Sessions; for though by *Stat.* 6 *E.* 1. *c.* 9.

M 3 and

and 4 *E.* 3. Murthers and other Homicides muſt ſtay till Gaol Delivery; yet the *Stat.* of 18 *E.* 3. *c.*2. 34 *E.* 3. *c.* 1. 17 *R.* 2. *c.* 10. hath enlarged their Commiſſion and Power.

Yet in reſpect the *Stat.* 1 & 2 *Ph.* & *Ma.c.* 13. directs Juſtices of Peace to take Examinations in Caſes of Homicide and other Felonies, and to certifie them to the Juſtices of Gaol Delivery: In point of Diſcretion they do forbear to proceed to determine great Felonies.

Dalt. c.20. But for Petit Larceny, and other ſmall Felonies, they uſe to bind over the Proſecutor to the Seſſions.

The Juſtices of Peace may proceed upon Indictments taken before themſelves, or former Juſtices of Peace: but cannot proceed upon Indictments before Coroner, or Oyer and Terminer; but Juſtices of Gaol Delivery may; and the Juſtices of Peace are to deliver the Indictments taken before them to the Juſtices of Gaol Delivery, by *Stat.* 4 *E.* 3. *c.* 2.

By *Stat.* 4 *E.* 3. *c.* 2.

They

They cannot deliver perſons ſuſ- Crom. fo. 9.
pect by Proclamation, as Juſtices of
Gaol Delivery may.

In Caſes of Felonies by *Statute*
limited to be heard before Juſtices
of Peace, they may proceed at Seſſions; and conſequently may bind
over Informers, and certifie Examina-
nations at Seſſions.

But ſuch *Felonies* by *Statute* as
are ſpecially limited to Juſtices of
Oyer and Terminer, or other Juſtices and not to them, the Juſtices of
Peace cannot proceed to take Indictments, as upon *Stat.* 3 *H.* 7.
c. 18. for contriving to deſtroy the
King, &c. upon *Stat.* 33 *H.* 8. *c.* 12.
Murtherers in the King's Palace;
upon *Stat.* 8 *H.* 6. *c.* 12. of razing
or imbezelling Records ; upon *Stat.*
5 *El. c.* of Forgery ; upon *Stat.*
13 *H.* 6. *c.* 1. ſecret imbezelling
goods, &c. up *Stat.* 2 & 3 *Ed.* 6.
c. 24. ſtriken in one City, and dies
in another, or acceſſory in another
County.

But in the former caſes it ſeems Dal. c.20.
they may take the Examinations,
and

and commit the Offenders, and bind over Profecutors.

If any Indictment be taken before Juftices of Oyer and Terminer, Gaol Delivery, or *Coroner*, they cannot proceed upon them; but upon Indictments taken before the Sheriff in his Turn, they may proceed by *Stat.* 1 *E.*4.*c.*2.

In cafes of Treafon, Mifprifion of Treafon or Premunire, regularly Juftices of Peace have no Jurifdiction; yet two things may be done:

Dal.c.90.
1. In any cafe of Treafon, becaufe it is a breach of the Peace, they may upon complaint imprifon Offenders, take Examinations, bind Profecutors over, and certifie their Proceedings into King's Bench or Gaol Delivery.

Dal.c.2.
2. In fome cafes they are enabled to take Indictments, but not to hear and determine the fame, but certifie the fame into the King's Bench, upon *Stat.* of 5 & 23 *El.*

1. Maintainer of Authority of the See of *Rome*.
2. Obtaining Bulls, &c.

3. With-

3. Withdrawing from Allegiance.

4. Bringing in *Agnus Dei*, &c.

A perſon bringing one before a Juſtice, ſuſpect of Felony, and refuſing to be bound to proſecute, may be Committed, if it appear he can teſtifie materially.

They may Enquire of any Felony within the County, though within the Verge. 4 *R.Wigg*'s Caſe.

Coroner.

Coroner.

HAth power in three Cases:
1. To take Indictments [of] Death; but this he can only d[o] *super visum corporis*, otherwise void Hence,

St.P.C. fo. 52.   1. If the Body be interred b[e]fore he come, the Townshi[p] amerced, and he must dig up the Body; so if th[e] Township suffer the Bod[y] to lie long to Putrefactio[n] without sending for the C[o]roner: The like of one dyin[g] in Prison.

2. If the Coroner be remiss and comes not being sen[t] for, he shall be fined an[d] imprisoned.

3. He may enquire of fligh[t] and such Presentment no[t] Traversable.

4. If the Body cannot be see[n] the Justices of the Peac[e] may enquire thereof.

Nota,

Nota, The Record of the Coroner
of great Authority; if he Record a
Confeſſion of a Felony by Approver,
[o]r a Confeſſion of breach of Priſon,
[or] an Abjuration, it ſhall not be Tra-
[ve]rſed.

5. *Jury dnt' Coroner acquit perſon
[in ca]ſe dnt' enquire quis occidit*, 11 E. 4.
14 H. 7. 2.

And it ſeems by ſome he hath
[po]wer to enquire of Rape, Breach
[of] Priſon.

He hath Juriſdiction upon Arms
[of] the Sea, where a man may ſee
[fro]m ſide to ſide.

2. Concerning *Appeals*.

The Coroner, together with the
[Sh]eriff, hath power in the County
[C]ourt to receive Appeals of Robbe- St.PC. fo. 52.
[ry] and other Felonies: But then it
[mu]ſt be of a Felony in the ſame
[C]ounty: Upon this Appeal they may
[gr]ant Proceſs till Utlary; but it ſeems
[th]ey cannot ſend an *Exigent*, becauſe
[pr]ohibited by *Stat.* of *Mag. Chart. c.* 17.

Such Appeal may be by Bill; and St.PC. fo. 64.
[it] may be removed into King's Bench
[by] *Certiorari*, but it muſt iſſue both

to

to Sheriff and Coroner, and not t[o]
Sheriff only.

It appears by *Stat.* 3 *H.* 7. *c.* 1. Th[at]
an Appeal of Murther by Bill, li[es]
before Sheriff and Coroner.

3. The Coroner alone may tal[e]
the Appeal of any *Approver* of
Felony in any County.

St.PC f.53.

But then he cannot make Proce[ss]
thereupon, but enter it in his Ro[ll]
and send it to the Justices of Ga[ol]
Delivery, who thereupon may iss[ue]
their Process to the Sheriff of t[he]
foreign County, to take the Appe[l]-
lee.

4. To take the *Abjuration* of hi[m]
that acknowledges a Felony done [in]
the same County, or any other.

And note, That though more C[o]-
roners than one in any County, y[et]
any one may exercise any of t[he]
Powers before.

But the Presentment of him th[at]
is first taken stands.

Sheri[ff]

Sheriff.

THe Power of the Sheriff to take Indictments, was either *virtute Commissionis*, which is taken away by the *Stat.* 28 *E.* 3. *c.* 9.

Officii; in his Turn: wherein,

1. The *Turns* must be held *infra ensem Paschæ & Michaelis*; otherwise the Indictments there are void per *Stat.* 31 *E.* 3. *c.* 14.

St. P.C. £48.

2. The Indictments must be under Seal of the Jury by *Statute* of *West.* 2. *c.* 13. indented *per Stat.* E. 3. *c.* 17. and the same for Lords of Franchises.

3. The Indictors must be of good fame, having 20 *s.* Freehold, or 26 *s.* 8 *d.* Copyhold; otherwise Sheriff punishable by *Stat.* 1 *R.* 3. *c.* 4.

4. The Turn can take no Indictment but of that which is Felony by Common Law, or of such Matters as are particularly by Act of Parliament limited to them, and therefore

fore an Indictment of Rape voi[d]
there.

5. Upon any Indictment of Felo[-]
ny before the Sheriff in his Turr[n]
they can make out no Process, bu[t]
muſt ſend them to the Juſtices [of]
Peace, who have power to proce[ed]
thereupon as if taken before then[-]
ſelves, by *Stat.* 1 *E* 4. *c.*2.

Court

Court-Leet.

THe *Court-Leet* hath in effect the same Jurisdiction with the Turn; but Presentments of Felony before them are to be sent before Justices of Gaol Delivery. 3 *H*.4.18.

The means of bringing Ca[pital] Offenders to Tria[l]

Having confidered the Cour[t] of Juftice, now we come t[o] confider the means of bringing C[a]pital Offenders to their Trial; an[d] that is Regularly by one of the three ways;

    Appeal.
    Approver.
    Indictment.

And herein fome things are prop[er] to each proceeding.

§. Some things are common [to] them all, which come to be con[si]dered after Particulars, proper [to] either, difpatched, *viz.*

    Procefs.
    Arraignment; and therein of Pri[n]cipal and Acceffory.
    Demeanour of the Party A[r]raigned;
                    Standin[g]

Standing Mute.
Confessing.
Pleading and Pleas.

   Declinatory,
   Sanctuary,
   Clergy.

In Bar,
   Pardon.
   Auterfoits Acquit.
   Auterfoits Convict.

To the Felony,
   Trial.
   By Battel.
   By Jury, and therein
   Procefs againſt the
      Jury.
   Challenge.
   Evidence.
   Verdict.
   By Peers, in cafe of
      Nobility.

178 Capital Offenders to trial.

Judgment in the several Cases Capital.

Execution.
Reprieve.
Falsifier.
By Error.
By Plea.

Appeal

Appeal.

Appeals in respect of the *manner* of proceeding, are of two kinds

1. By Writ.
2. By Bill.

Touching Appeals *by Bill*, they may be prosecuted.

1. In the King's Bench against any that is *in custodia Marescalli*, or let to bail: they are the Sovereign Coroners.
2. In the Court before Commissioners of Gaol Delivery against a Prisoner, or one let to bail, but not, of one let to Mainprize.

But if one of the Appellees absent, remove in *B.R.* by *Certiorari*.

3. By some other Justices of Peace, *quod Quære* 44 *E*. 3. *Coron* 95.
4. Before Sheriff and Coroner, as before; and it may be removed by *Certiorari* in *B.R*. 3 *H*.7. *c*. 1.

5. Be-

Appeal.

5. Before the Conſtable and Mar-
ſhal, of a Felony done out of the
Realm, 1 *H*.4.*c*.14.

In relation to the *Matter*.
Appeals are in Matter,

1. *Not Capital*, as an Appeal of
Maihem, which may be commenced
in King's Bench, Gaol Delivery, or
before Coroner and Sheriff.

This, though it be *felonice*, yet is
but a Treſpaſs in its Nature and Judgment.

2. *Capital*; and that either,
　1. Of *Treaſon*; but this ouſted
　　by *Stat.* 1 *H*.4.*c*.14.
　2. Of *Felony*; and theſe of three
　　kinds:
　　　1. Of Death.
　　　2. Of Larceny.
　　　3. Of Rape.

Appeal of Death.

AN Appeal *of Death* is either by the Wife or Heir.
1. Appeal of Death *by the Wife*; and therein thefe *requifite:*
    1. She ought to be a Wife *de jure*, and not *de facto* only; and therefore *ne unque accouple* a good Plea.
    2. But fhe need not be dowable; for if fhe had Eloped, or the Husband been Attaint; yet fhe may have an Appeal of his death.
    3. She ought to continue his Widow; for if fhe marry before, or pending the Appeal, the Appeal fails for ever; or if fhe marry after Judgment, fhe cannot have Execution.
2. Appeal of Death *by the Heir.*
    1. If the dead hath a Wife, the Heir fhall not have Appeal though fhe die within the year: But if the Wife

Appeal.

kill the Husband, there the Heir shall have an Appeal.

2. He must be Heir by course of Common Law; this hath these Exceptions:
   1. Where Heir is disabled by Attainder.
   2. Where the Appeal is against the Heir; in these cases i[t] goes to the next Heir, as i[f] the other were dead withou[t] Issue.
3. It must be by Heir that wa[s] Heir at time of death [of] Ancestor; for if he di[e] within the year before, o[r] after Appeal commenced, [it] is lost.

But it seems, if the Heir havin[g] Judgment die, his Heir ma[y] have Execution.

4. It must be an Heir an[d] Male; *Nullus capiatu[r] propr' Appellum fœmin[æ] alterius quam viri sui:* Bu[t] if he be Heir, and Mal[e] though he derive throug[h] Female[.]

Females, he may have an C. Lit.
Appeal.

5. A man above *Seventy*, or an Infant, may have Appeal; but no Battel waged, and adjudged of late times the Parol shall not Demur. *Sed Quære.*

But an Idiot, Monk, or Man mute, shall have no Appeal, neither of death, nor otherwise.

And Note, the Appeal of death C.PC.53. must be within year and day after death by *Stat.* 3 *E.* 6. *c.*24. striken in one County, and dies in another; or Accessory in one County, to death in another: Appeal brought where party died.

Appeal

Appeal of Robbery.

Servant robbed, Master or Servant may have Appeal.

But Testator robbed, Executors shall not have Appeal.

Villain shall not have Appeal of Robbery against his Lord; *contra* of Death.

Two joint Owners robbed, Survivor shall have Appeal.

A Woman or Infant shall have an Appeal of Robbery.

If a man be robbed at several times, he must put all into one Appeal.

What omitted is Confiscate.

The Appeal affirms the continuation of the property. Therefore if *A.* rob *B.* in the County of *S.* and go with the Goods into the County of *D.* an Appeal of Larceny lies in the County of *D.* but not of Robbery, for that is upon a taking from the person.

If *A.* be robbed by *B.* who is robbed by *C. A.* may have an Appeal of Larceny against *C.*

This

This Appeal may be prosecuted in a year, two, or three, if there was fresh Suit; and the judging of fresh Suit lies in the discretion of the Court.

And Note, This, or any other Appeal lies against an Infant, against a Monk, without naming his Sovereign, against a Feme covert without naming her Husband.

Appeal of Rape.

Appeal of Rape.
1. Lies for the party ravished.
2. But if she consented to th[e] Rape afterwards, then by *Stat.*6 [H] 2. *c.* it is given to the Husband ; [if] none, to the Father; if none, to th[e] Heir, whether Male or Female.

If she be taken in one County and ravished in another, the Appe[al] of Rape lies in that County whe[re] actually ravished.

Although by *Stat. W.* 1. *c.* 1[3] whereby Rape was turned into Tre[s]pass, forty days is limited for h[er] Suit; yet it being again made Felon[y] by *Stat. W.* 2. *c.* and no time limite[d] for it, it may be brought in any re[a]sonable time.

Proces[s]

Procefs in Appeal.

Concerning Procefs in Appeals, *vi. infra* Procefs in general, becaufe many things therein common to Appeals and Indictments.

The *Count* in an Appeal.

1. The Plaintiff in his Appeal muft mention the place and day; need not mention the hour; and though day be miftaken, not material upon Evidence.
2. It fufficeth for Plaintiff to count againft Defendant, according to the conftruction that the Law maketh upon the Fact.
If *A. B.* and *C.* prefent, and *B.* only ftrike the mortal ftroke, he may count againft them all, that they ftrook: So in Rape.
3. An Appeal by Heir ought to hew *Coment.*
4. In Appeal of Rape, *felonice rapuit* fufficient, without faying *carnaliter cognovit*, vid. 11 *H*.4.1.

5. In

5. In Appeal against *A.B.* and *C. A* only appears, he must count against all by the better Opinion.

6. At this day but one Appeal against all Principals and Accessories, and if an Appeal be against *A.* and he is attaint or acquit, or Plaintiff non-suit, he cannot have another Appeal against *B.* But if Accessory in one County to Felony in another there several Appeals against Principal and Accessories.

Appeal.

Pleas to the Writ and in Bar.

Writ of Appeal abate,
1. For insufficiency in the Writ, is wanting *rapuit*, false Latin, &c.
2. Multiplicity of Action; a second Writ of Appeal purchased, pending a former Writ abates; but if pending a former in the County abates not.

But if the first Appeal by Bill be removed into the Bench by *Certiorari*, and the Plaintiff had appeared thereupon, and counted, abates the second Writ.

Nul tiel in rerum natura, as one of the Defendants, abates *vers touts*, &c.

Appeal.

Pleas in Bar.

Vid. infra in ceo general Title, as t[o] *Autrefoits Convict* or *Acquit*.

C.P.C. 98.   1. He may plead any thin[g] whereby it appears the Plaintiff [is] not intituled to the Appeal, *de q[uo] v. supra*.

2. Nonsuit in a former Appe[al] after Declaration, so of a *Retraxit*.

3. The Plaintiff brought an A[p]peal of the same Felony against an[o]ther, who was acquit or attaint at h[is] Suit.

4. Plaintiff hath released to D[e]fendant; but if Appeal against D[i]vorce, a Release or *Retraxit* as [to] one, no bar for the other.

5. If Defendant plead in Bar, [he] may also plead over to the Felon[y] and it shall not be double.

    1. But in case of a Relea[se] pleaded, he shall not plea[d] over to the Felony, becau[se] repugnant.

2. In case of Villenage pleaded he shall not plead to the Felony, because Infranchisement; yet if that bar found against him, he may plead Not Guilty; and so in any other case where he pleads in bar without pleading over, except Release.

Approver.

Approver.

C.PC.c.65.
S.PC. f.142.

1. What it is to be an Approver?
A person indicted of Treason o[r] Felony not disabled to accuse befor[e] competent Judges, confessing th[e] Indictment, and sworn to reveal a[ll] Treasons and Felonies he know[s] and then before a Coroner entrin[g] his Appeal against *participes Cri[-]minis* in the Indictment within th[e] Realm.

2. Who may be an Approver, an[d] who not?
   1. A Peer of the Realm canno[t] be an Approver.
   2. A person Attaint cannot b[e] an Approver; nor a pe[r]son out of Prison, thoug[h] indicted.
   3. A Woman, Infant, Idiot *Non compos*, Clerk, canno[t] be Approver.
   4. But a Man above seventy, or maimed may, but h[e] shall not wage Battel.
   5. Clerl[

Approver.   193

    5. Clerk Convict may.
3. In what cases?
    1. None can approve but an indicted; and therefore if only in Prison upon suspicion, he may indeed confess the Felony, but such Confession amounteth not to an Attainder or Conviction, though it be an Evidence, and therefore cannot approve.
    2. The Appellee in Appeal cannot be an Approver.
    3. Appellee of Approver cannot be Approver, for that would be infinite.
    4. Though a person Indicted approve, yet if after an Appeal be against him, the Approvement ceaseth.
    5. He that hath once pleaded to the Felony cannot be Approver, but shall be hanged, for he is found false.
4. Of what Offences?

It muſt be only of the Offences contained in the Indictment, be it Felony or Treaſon, and therefore not of another Offence, nor of an Acceſſory before or after to the ſame Offence; yet his Oath general therefore as to other Offences, it is but a Detection, not an approvement.

5. Before whom?

Before ſuch Judges only as can aſſign a Coroner, as King's Bench Gaol Delivery, Oyer and Terminer High Steward; but not before Juſtices of Peace, Court Baron, or County Court.

But it is in the diſcretion of the Court either to ſuffer him to be Approver, or to reſpit Judgment and Execution, till he hath Convicted all his Partners.

6. How Demeſned after Appeal?

1. After Felony confeſſed upon the Arraignment, a Coroner aſſigned and ſworn in Court to diſcover Offenders.

2.

2. A day prefix'd, within which he is to perfect his Appeal before the Coroner, and in every of those days he must Appeal; for if he fail in any, and the Coroner record it, he is to be hanged.

The time limited to perfect his Appeal by 5 *E.* 2. *c.* 34. is three days, but that Repealed 15 *E.*2.

3. During the time limited for his Appeal, he shall be at large, and have 1 *d. per diem* till his Appeal finished.

4. If he Appeal persons beyond Sea, or such as are not in *rerum natura*, and that appear by Testimony of Country, or by Return of Sheriff *quod non fuit invent'*, he shall be hanged.

5. After his Appeal formed before the Coroner, he must repeat it *verbatim* before the Court; and if he fail thereof,

thereof, and the Coroner Record it, he shall be hanged.

7. *Process* in Appeal.
1. In the same County the Coroner may award Process to the Sheriff, till Exigent.
2. If Appellee be in a foreign County, then the Judges before whom the Appeal is, may grant Process, *viz. B. R.* or *Itinerant* by Common Law; and by *Statute* of 28 *Ed.* 1. *de Appellatis*, the Justices of Gaol Delivery may send Process into a Foreign County, as well to apprehend the Appellee, as a *Venire facias* to try the Issue.

S. P. C. f. 146.

8. *Proceeding* upon *Trial.*
The Appellee may put himself upon the Country, or wage Battel.

If five Appellees, and they wage Battel, he must fight them all.

If two Approvers against one Appellee, if the Appellee vanquish the first, he is acquitted against the rest though

though Appellor retract his Appeal, or be vanquished; yet if the Offence be within Clergy, he shall have it; and so of the Appellee.

9. *Proceeding after Trial.*

If the Appellor convict the Appellee, either by Battel or Verdict, the King *ex merito justitiæ* is to pardon him; and from the time of his Appeal till his Pardon or Conviction, ought to have wages.

Indictments.

These things considerable:
1. Where an Indictment requisite in cases Capital, and where not.
2. What the quality of Indictors.
3. Of what Matters they may Enquire.
4. Before whom found.
5. What requisite in the manner of them.

1. Where an Indictment requisite for a party to be Arraigned at the King's Suit.

1. By the Ancient Law, if a man was taken in Larceny with the manner, and that brought into Court with the Prisoner, the Prisoner should be Arraigned thereupon without any Indictment. *Stat. P.C.* *f.*148.

And such was the use of those Manors that had Infangthef. *Ibid.* *f.*29. *Vid.* 1 *E.* 3. 17. 17 *Aſſ.* 49. but this difused.

2. If

Indictments.

2. If Trespass be brought *de mu-* S.PC.f.94.
liere abducta cum bonis viri, and the
Defendant found Guilty: Or if in
Trespass for Goods the Defendant
be found that he stole them; this in
the King's Bench equivalent to an
Indictment, and the Defendant put
to answer to the Felony.

3. In some Cases upon Appeals,
by Appellors or Approvers not prosecuting, &c. the Defendant arraigned at the King's Suit; because
it carries a presumption of Truth;
and therefore if the Defendant be
both Appealed and Indicted upon a
Non-prosecution of the Appeal, the
party shall be arraigned upon the Appeal, not the Indictment. 4 *E*.4.10.

Wherein,

1. If the Plaintiff in Appeal by S.PC. f.148.
Writ be Nonsuit before Declaration, he shall not be arraigned at the
King's Suit. 1. Because no certainty. 2. The Writ may be at anothers Suit, but if it be by Bill either by Appellor or Approver, it
seems he shall, because the certainty
appears; therefore in the former
Case,

Indictments.

Case, if there be no Indictment against him, he is dismissed.

2. If the Plaintiff release his Appeal after he hath commenced it, the party shall be arraigned at King's Suit: But if before it was commenced, then not; because it was never well commenced.

3. If the Plaintiff or Approver, after Appeal commenced, confess it false, or take to his Clergy, or wave his Appeal, yet arraigned at the Suit of the King: But if the Approver after Battel joyned do in the field confess it false, the Appellor hang'd, and the Appellee discharged, because amounts to a vanquishment.

4. If the Appeal abate by Act of the Plaintiff, as taking Husband; or act in Law, as death; Appellee arraigned at the King's Suit: But if it abate by insufficiency in the Appeal, as by false Latin, Misnosmer, or because Plaintiff disabled to commence Appeal, as Utlary of Felony, or Trespass; or the year and day past; or Plaintiff not Wife or Heir; Defendant, not arraigned upon Appeal, but may be Indicted. 2. If

5. If the King pardon after Battel joyned in Appeal by Approver, no Arraignment at King's Suit, but Appellee difcharged.

And Note, where the Prifoner arraigned upon the Appeal, a *Ceſſet Proceſſus* entred upon the Indictment. St.PC.104.

The Retorn of the Sheriff of Refcue or Efcape of a Felon, not fufficient to put the party to anfwer the Felony. S. PC.

2. The fecond thing confiderable, is the quality of *the Indictor*.

Concerning Indictments in Leets and Turns, *vide ante* upon *Stat.* *V.* 2. *c.* 13. 1 *E* 3. *c.* 17. 1 *R.* 3. *c.* 4. 1 *E.* 4. . 3.

There is a General *Statute* that refers to all Indictors, as well in cafe of Felony as Treafon, 11 *H.* 4. *c.* 9. which requires, St.PC. f. 33.

1. Indictors not to be,
   1. Perfons fled to Sanctuary for Felony or Treafon.
   2. Not Outlawed.
   3. Not Indicted or Attainted.
   4. Not by Confpiracy.

2. That

Indictments.

2. That the Indictors be the King's Liege People.

3. Returned by the Sheriff, or Bailiffs of Franchises.

4. Not at the nomination of any person.

And all Indictments taken contrary void.

Hence it follows:

1. That the Prisoner upon his Arraignment may plead this matter or any Point of the *Statute*, and may plead over to the Felony. *Vid Scarlet*'s Case.

2. Though there be twenty of the Grand Jury, yet if one was outlawed or taken at the nomination of another, it avoids the whole Indictment.

By *Stat.* 3 *H.* 8. *c.* 12. Justices of Gaol Delivery, or of Peace, whereof one of the *Quorum*, in open Sessions, may reform the Panel of the Grand Jury, by putting in and taking out Names, and the Sheriff is to return the Pannel so reformed.

But this takes not away the former *Statute* of 11 *H.* 4 nor alters it

By

By *Stat.* 33 *H*.6.c.2.
Special provision is made for the [q]uality of the Indictors in *Lanca*[s]hire.

3. Of which things they can Enquire.

Regularly they can Enquire of [n]othing but what ariseth within the [B]ody of the County, for which they [a]re retorned.

And therefore if an Indictment [fo]r Scandalous Words, or other matt[e]r transitory be found upon Not [G]uilty pleaded thereunto, if upon [E]vidence it appear to be spoken in [a]nother County, the Defendant is [n]ot guilty.

And therefore where Stroke was [in] one County, and Death in ano[th]er, he could not be Indicted where [p]arty died.

But for a Nusance in one County [to] another, a Jury of the County [w]here Nusance is committed may [In]dict it.

But divers *Statutes* have Intro[d]uced an alteration of the Law in [so]me Capital Cases, 28 *H.* 8. c. 15.
Treas

Indictments.

Treasons, Felonies, Robberies, Murthers and Confederacies upon the Sea may be enquired, tried, heard, determined, and judged in such Shires and places as shall be limited by the King's Commission to be directed for the same.

A Treason done out of the Land it hath been held that it may be enquired of and tried where the Offender had Lands; but to avoid the Question by *Stat.* 35 *H*.8. *c*. 2. al Treasons and Misprisions, or concealments of Treasons done out of *England*, may be enquired, heard and determined by the Justices o the King's Bench, by persons of the County where the Bench sits, o before Commissioners, and in such Shires as shall be appointed by the King's Commission, by good men of the same Shire, as if the Treasons,&c. had been done in the same Shire where inquired.

Upon this *Statute*.

St. PC.f.71.

1. If the Bench remove after Indictment into another County, the Trial shall be by persons of the first County. 2. The

2. The King's writing his Name to the Commiſſion, or putting his Signature to the Warrant, ſufficient.

3. *Ireland* is out of the Realm to this purpoſe.

Theſe *Statutes* ſtand unrepealed by *Stat.* of 1 *Ma.c.* but the *Stat.* of 32 *H.*8. *c.*4. for trial of Treaſon in Wales, repealed by 1 *Ma.* C.PC. f.14.

Again, by *Stat.* 2 & 3 *El. c.* 24. A man ſtricken in the County of *D.* dies in the County of *S.* or Acceſſory in one County to Felony in another County, may be indicted and tried in the County where the death was, or Felony committed by the Principal; but it muſt be laid according to truth. C.PC. 49.

If Inqueſt conceal any matter preſentable before Juſtice of Peace, they may impannel Inqueſt to enquire of ſuch Concealments, and amerce the Concealers, by *Stat.* 3 *H. c.* 1.

4. Before whom found.
    Of this before.

5. The

Indictments.

St. PC.

5. The form of Indictments.
1. By *Statutes*:
4 *H.*4 *c.*2. *Infidiatores viarun & depopulatores agrorum*, t(be omitted in Indictments and if inserted, yet Clerg) not thereby taken away.
37 *H.* 8. *c.* 8. Indictment nc to be quashed for want c the words, *viz. gladiis, ba culis, & cultellis.*
2. At Common Law :
1. Want of certainty vitiates want of year, day and place.

Indictment for Escape of one ta ken on suspicion of Felony, withou shewing what Felony, *Male.*

Indictment for receipt of a Felor without shewing who received, *Mal*

Indictment *ad magnam Curiam (Letam, Male.*

Indictment for making Alchim *ad inftar pecuniæ Regis*, withou shewing what Mony, *Male.*

Indictment *quod communis Mal. factor*, without shewing wherein *Male.*

Indictment *quod cepit*, or *furatu eft*

ſt, without ſaying *felonice* ; *abduxit quum*, without ſaying *cepit* ; or *carnaliter cognovit*, without ſaying *Rauit* ; or *burgariter*, when it ſhould be *Burglariter*; or if Felony before Juſtice of Peace, without ſaying *necnon ad diverſas felonias, &c.* or before the Mayor of *London* without ſaying *& Coronatore* ; or of a Murther with a Gun, without ſaying *Percuſſit, Male*.

Indictment ſuppoſing the Stroak, *Auguſti*, death 2 *Auguſti*, *& ſic felonice murdravit* 1 *Auguſti*, *Male*. But *ſic murdravit modo & forma præd'*, or *præd'* 2 *Auguſti*, *Bene*.

Indictment, *quod dedit mortalem plagam circa pectus, Male*: But, *in ſiniſtra parte ventris circa umbelicum, Bene*.

Indictment *de morte cujuſdam ignoti*, or *felonice cepit bona, &c. cujuſdam ignoti*, or *domus & Eccleſiæ*, time of Vacation, good.

Indictment of Poyſoning with ſeveral ſorts of Poyſon, without ſhewing of which he died: good. C. PC. c. 62.

6. *Proof*

6. *Proof upon Indictments.*

In cafe of Treafon and Mifprifion by the *Stat.* 1 *E.* 6. *c.* 12. & 5 *E.* 6. *c.* 11. there ought to be two lawfu[l] Accufers, that is, Witneffes upo[n] every Indictment.

C.PC.24. An Accufer by hearfay, is no lawful Accufer within this *Statute.*

The neceffity of fuch Proof upo[n] Indictment of Treafon, is not take[n] away by *Stat.* 1 *E.* 1. 2. 1 & 2 *P[h]* & *Ma.c.* 11. but only in the cafe [of] counterfeiting Coin.

St.PC.164. But thefe Witneffes need not b[e] prefent with the Indictors, but the[y] may fend it to them in writing.

Process.

NOw we come to thofe Proceedings that for the moſt part are common both to Appeals and Indictments. And,
1. Of *Process.*
    1. Upon an Indictment or Appeal *of Death* but one *Capias*, and then *Exigent:* but in caſe of Robbery, then by *Stat.* 25 *E.* 3. *c.* 14. two *Capias's*, then *Exigent*; but this *Stat.* extends not to death.
    2. But Indictments or Appeals of Treaſon, or any Felony, or Treſpaſs *againſt a perſon of another County* after one *Cap'* a ſecond *Cap'* with Proclamations, ſhall be granted to the Sheriff of that County wherein he is ſuppoſed to be converſant before an *Exigent* ſhall iſſue by *Stat.* 8 *H.*6. *c.* 10. And upon

upon this *Statute* Process shall go to a County Palatine; and if in the Indictment he be styled *nuper de D.* and so in several Counties, the second *Cap'* shall go to every County.

S.PC. f.67.
3. In Appeal or Indictment *against Principal and Accessory*, by *Stat. W.* 1. *c.* 14. Process of Utlary must stay against Accessory till Principal attaint.

But if it be an Appeal *by Writ* which is general till Declaration, the Plaintiff must at his peril distinguish the Process; for if he take his *Exigent* against all, he must Count against all as Principals.

An Appeal *against divers*, one appears and pleads to the Writ, or in Bar, which goes to all, Process of Utlary shall stay against the rest till Plea determined.

An

Process.

An Indictment or Appeal may be *removed* in *B. R.* by *Certiorari*, but it must accord with the Appeal.

Upon an Appeal removed by *Certiorari*, the Plaintiff is without day; and to compel the Plaintiff to proceed, the Defendant may take out a *Scire facias*, and upon two *Nihils* or a *Scire feci*, and default, Defendant discharged.

But the Plaintiff upon such Appeal removed, may have *Capias* & *Exigent*.

If the Defendant comes in by *Capias*, and after appearance make default, a new *Capias*; if upon *Exigent*, a new *Exigent*; and upon second appearance shall plead *de novo*, for the first Issue and Inquest is *sine die*.

Arraignment.

1. IN what *manner* a Perſon is to be Arraigned?

The Priſoner, at the time of his Arraignment ought not to be in Irons.

St. PC. f. 66.

2. Where arraigned *upon ſeveral Appeals or Indictments.*

If a man be indicted or appealed of Robbery or Death at the Suit of one, he ſhall be arraigned and tried at the Suit of another, becauſe they have ſeveral intereſts in the Judgments.

And now the ſame Law is of an Indictment of Robbery, becauſe by *Stat.* 21 *H.* 8. *c.* 11. the party is to have Reſtitution.

But if the Appeal by one be not commenced till after an Attainder at the Suit of another, he ſhall not be arraigned upon the other Suit:

But if the firſt Attainder be pardoned, he ſhall be arraigned upon the

Arraignment.

the second Appeal commenced after the Attainder.

But after an Attainder of Felony, he may be arraigned for Treason for the King's Interest.

By the Common Law, a Clerk convict should have answered all Felonies, and were acquit or convict at the Suit of others.

But this was remedied by *Stat.* 25 *E.*3.*c.*4. *pro Clero.* And therefore after that *Statute*, the Clerk convict and delivered to the Ordinary, was discharged of all former Felonies whereof he was not arraigned before Clergy; and that although those other Offences were not within Clergy. *Dyer* 214.

But now by *Stat.* 8 *El. c.* 4. after Purgation, and 18 *El.c.*7. after burning in the Hand, he shall be put to answer former Felonies upon Appeal or Indictment. *Vid. infra in auterfoits acquit & convict.*

3. Concerning the *Arraignment of Principal and Accessory.*

1. Who

Arraignment.

1. Who shall be said an Accessory
   Before,
   After.
2. How the Proceeding shall be against them upon their Arraignment.

Principal and Accessory.

1. **Who an *Accessory*?**

    1. In Treason no Accessories, C. PC. f. 138. but all Principals: But a Procurer before, or a Receiver knowingly after, is guilty as Principal in High Treason.
    2. Where an Act of Parliament C. PC. f. 59. makes a Felony, it doth incidently make such Accessories as would be Accessories before or after to a Felony at Common Law; as in case of Buggery, Rape, &c.
    3. The Accessory cannot be guilty of Petit Treason, where the Principal is but Murther.
    4. If divers come to commit an unlawful act, and be present at the time of Felony committed, though one of them only doth it, they are all Principals.

So if one present move the other to strike: Or if one present did nothing, but yet came to assist party if need: Or if one hold the party while the Felon strikes him: Or if one present deliver his Weapon to the other that strikes; for they are *præsentes, auxiliantes, abettantes,* or *confortantes.*

S.P.C.f.40. But if one came casually, not of the Confederacy, though he hindered not the Felony, he is neither Principal nor Accessory, although he apprehend not the Felon.

5. In some cases a person *absent* may be Principal.

4 Rep.44.
Vauxe's case.
C.P.C.138.
1. He that puts Poison into any thing to poison another, and leaves it, though not present when taken: And so it seems are all that are present when the Poison is so infused, and consenting thereto.

2. If upon the same Ground, or in the same House, though not within view of the Fact, when many come

Principal and Accessory.

ome to do an unlawful act: See efore Lord *Dacre*'s Case, and *Pudsy*'s Case in Murther and Robbery.

3. By special Act of Parliament, s upon the *Stat.* 3 *H.* 7. c. 2. 8 *H.* 6. 2.

2. Accessories *before*; he that ommandeth or assenteth to the ommitting of a Felony, and is abnt when done.

1. In Manslaughter there can be Accessory before, because done ithout premeditation. 4 Rep. *Bibith*'s case.

2. Where the Execution varies om the Command in the person in; as a Command to kill *A.* and kill *B.* or in the nature of the Offnce; as Command to rob *A.* as he es to Market, and he break open s House and robs it, the Comman- r is not Accessory. C.P.C. f. 57.

3. But a Command to poison *J. S.* d he shoots him; a Command to b or beat *J. S.* and he beats him death, the Commander Accesso-

4. If *A.* Command *B.* to kill *C.* d before the Fact *A.* repents, and
count-

countermands his Command, yet B kills him, *A.* is not Acceſſory.

5. If *A.* poiſon an Apple, and deliver it to *C.* to deliver to *D C.* not knowing delivers it, Murther in *A.* but no Offence in *C.*

3. Acceſſory *after.*

St.PC.41.

1. A Receipt of ſtolen Good makes not Acceſſory, unleſs he receive Thief. *Ou recieve le biens auter Felon,* 9 H.4.1.

2. Every Receipt to make an Acceſſory, muſt be knowing him to b ſuch.

But if a man be attaint of Felony in the County of *A.* the Law preſumes Notice thereof in the ſam County: Therefore the Receipt of him in the ſame County ſeems Acceſſory; *Contra,* if in another County. *Videtur cognitio requiſita i utroque.*

3. Receit of a Felon, that hat given Bond to appear at Seſſions,&c not Acceſſory.

4. Relieving a Felon with Mony, Victuals, Horſe for his Journey
know

Principal and Accessory.

nowing Accessory: But if he be in
rison, then lawful. *Dal. c.*108.

5. A Brother receiving his Brother may be Accessory; or a Husband
and his Wife, but not the Wife of
her Husband.

6. A man may be Accessory to
an Accessory: And

The same man may be Principal
and Accessory where Felony done
by divers.

7. But sending a Letter in favour
of a Felon, instructing him to read,
advising to labour Witnesses not to
appear, not revealing a Felony intended, permitting a Felon to escape
without arrest, makes no Accessory:
sed Contempt.

8. Accessory cannot be unless a
Felony committed; therefore *A.*
wounds *B.* dangerously, *C.* receives
him, then *B.* dies, *C.* is not Accessory.

9. *Si*

9. *Si Felon vient al meason* J. S. *que suffer luy d'aler hors, n'est Felony, nisi prist Mony ou autre chose pur luy suffer Escape.* 9 H. 4. 1.

Arraign-

Arraignment of the Principal and Accessory, and things Observable therein.

1. IF the Principal be acquitted, or be convict only of Manslaughter, or *Se defendendo*, or before Attainder hath his Clergy, or be pardoned, or die, the Accessory shall not be arraigned; otherwise if after Attainder. S.PC. 47. C. PC. 139. 4 R. Seyer's case.

2. If the Principal be attaint at the Suit of the King, the Accessory shall not be arraigned at the Suit of the party. *Issint si soit attaint d'auter Felony.* S.PC. 47.

3. If Principal stand mute, Accessory not Arraigned. *Vid. Contra* R. 3. 22. 3 H. 7. 1.

4. The *Exigent* shall not go out against Accessory till Principal attaint by *Stat. W.* 1. c. 14. St. PC. 47.

5. Where

5. Where Principal appears not Acceſſory ſhall be put to anſwer; but he ſhall not be tried till Principal attaint or appear, unleſs he will for he may wave the benefit of the Law.

St. PC. 47.   6. If he be indicted as Acceſſory to two, and one of the Principals appears and is convict, the Court
Com. too.   may, if they pleaſe, try the Ac-
Gittin's caſe.   ceſſory; and if he be found Acceſſory to him that is attaint he ſhall be Condemned; if not found Acceſſory to him, yet he may after be Arraigned as Acceſſory to the other when he appears.

C. Weſt. 1. *c.* 14.   7. If Principal and Acceſſory appear and plead to the Felony, they may be tried by the ſame Inqueſt: but the Principal muſt be firſt Convict, and have Judgment, before Judgment againſt Acceſſory, and the Jury ſhall be [Charged] that if they find Principal not guilty, they ſhall find the Acceſſory not guilty.

8. If Principal be Erroneouſly attainted, yet Acceſſory ſhall not take

take advantage thereof, but be Arraigned.

9. If Murther or other Offence were in one County, and Accessory in another, by *Stat.* 2 *E.* 6. 24.

1. If Accessory be in *Middlesex*, where the King's Bench sits, and Principal in another County, the King's Bench may try the Accessory. C. PC p.49.

2. Certificate in such case shall be upon a *Certiorari* or Special Writ, and need be formed upon the Matter, and not by Precept, under their Seals, in their own Names. Ibid.

3. The High Steward is within the Act.

Accessory al Petit Larceny, 3 Cr. 50. *nemy al Homicide per infortun'*, 5 *E.*3. Coron. 116.

Novel Felony fait per Stat. vide nul Accessory nisi specialment enact e, Vid Dy. 88. Stam. 44.

Vid. pur Trial d' Accessory in foreign County. 2 E.6.cap.24. Dy.253.

Acquit

Acquit come Principal nemy arrain
come Accessory: Mes acquit come Ac-
cessory arrain come Principal.

Mute, *Paine fort & dure*.

<small>V. Stat. West. 1. cap. 12. & estre inquiry de offence dnt' *Paine fort & dure*.</small>

Now we come *to the Demeanor of the Prisoner* upon his appearance :
And thereupon either,
   1. He stands Mute.
   2. He pleads.
   3. Or he confesseth the Fact.
 1. What said a *standing Mute* ?
   This of two kinds :
   1. When he answers nothing at all: and then it shall be enquired, whether he stand Mute by malice or by the act of God. <small>W:st 1 .c.12. St.PC.f.150.</small>

If it be by the act of God, then the Felony shall be enquired of, and whether he be the same person, as if he had pleaded not guilty.

If by Malice, or if the Prisoner hath cut out his own Tongue, then he shall have Penance.

Nota, *Si ad unfoits pled' al Felony licet*

licet apres eſtoit Mute, ſer' trie, 15 E. 4. 33.

Viez Pere eſtoit Mute aver' Penance, 7 *Car.* Lord *Caſtlehaven*'s Caſe.

2. When he pleads, but not effectually; as when he anſwers not directly to the Fact, or concludes not upon the County, then if the cauſe be probable, he ſhall be put to his Penance. *C.PC.p.*227.

Nota, Si Chall' ultra 35. Standing Mute. *Vid.C.PC.fo.*227.

2. What *the Conſequent* of ſtanding Mute? 1. *Forfeit biens,* 14 E. 4. 7.

1. In Treaſon it is a Conviction.

2. After Attainder and ask'd what he can ſay why no Execution, ſtanding Mute he ſhall be Executed.

3. In Appeal ſtanding Mute, Judgment againſt him to be hanged. *Contra,* 14 *E.*4.1.

4. Upon *Stat.* 33 *H.* 8. *c.* 2. of Felony within the Verge, Offender ſtanding Mute, Judgment againſt him.

5. But

5. But in other cases of Felony, *Paine fort & dure*, and forfeits Goods.

   1. Remanded to Prison.

   2. Lie naked in some dark Room, with Hands and Legs extended.

   3. Weights increased.

Pleas.

IF the Prisoner plead, it is either,
   1. Declinatory.
      Sanctuary.
      Clergy.
   2. Or to the Felony:
      1. Demurring.
      2. Pleading in Bar.
      3. Pleading the General Issue.

Declinatory Exceptions:
1. *Sanctuary* and the Consequents, *Abjuration* ousted by *Stat.* 21 *Jac.* c.28.

Clergy.

Clergy.

2. *Clergy*, wherein
   1. Who shall have benefit of Clergy?
   2. In what Cases?
   3. At what time?
   4. Who the Judge?
   5. What the Consequent?

1. *Who* shall have Clergy, and who not?

   1. A Blind man shall not have his Clergy. *Nec* Jew, *nec* Turk: *Contr' de* Greek *ou home exçommeng'*.

   2. A Woman cannot have the benefit of Clergy.

Provision by *Stat.* 21 *Jac. c.* 6. C. P.C. c. 124. that for stealing Goods under 10 s. without Burglary or Robbery, &c. shall be Burnt in the Hand for the first Offence.

   3. Bigamy ousted of Clergy by *Stat. de Bigamis* 4 *E* 1. but restored to it by *Stat.* 1 *E* 6. *c.* 12.

Cestuy que abjure aver' Clergy apres son returne, 8 H. 8. Kel. 186.
Cestuy que ad unfoits Clergy n'aver' auterfoits, nisi deins Orders, 4 H. 7. c. 17.

2. *In what cases ?* Some things premised in general.

1. By *Stat.* 25 *E.* 3. *c.* 4. *pro Clero.* Clergy allowed in all Treasons or Felonies, except *Treason against the King; so that after that Statute,* there was Clergy in all Cases, but

$$\left\{\begin{array}{l}\text{Treason,}\\ \text{Sacrilege.}\end{array}\right.$$

2. Consequently wheresoever Clergy is not allowable in any other cases, it is taken away by some Act of Parliament.

3. Consequently where any Felony is made by a new *Stat.* Clergy is to be allowed, unless expresly taken away.

4. Con-

4. Consequently where by any special Act of Parliament Clergy is taken away in any Offence, the Indictment ought to bring the Case within the *Statute*. As upon the *Stat*. 3 & 4 *Ph.* & *Ma.* *c*. 4. the Indictment must run *Malitiose*; so upon *Stat.* 8 *El. c.* 4. it must be *clam & secrete*; in case of Murther, *ex malitia præcogitata*, otherwise Clergy allowable.
5. Consequently a *Statute* taking away Clergy from the Principal, doth not thereby take it from the Accessories before, unless specially provided for.
6. Where Clergy is allowable, it is to be allowed though the party be Convict by Confession, Verdict, or stands Mute, or challenges peremptorily above 35.

Clergy.

2. *Particular Offences* where Clergy, and where not.
  1. High *Treason* no Clergy.
  2. In Petit Treason. Principal ouſt of Clergy, if convict by Verdict or Confeſſion by *Stat.* 23 *H.* 8. *c.* 1. revived by 5 & 6 *E.* 6. *c.* 10. and by *Stat.* 25 *H.* 8. *c.* 3. though ſtanding Mute, not directly anſwering, or challenging above Twenty.
  Not ouſt of Clergy in Appeal, unleſs Convict by Verdict or Confeſſion.
  Acceſſories before the Fact maliciouſly, ouſt of Clergy in all caſes, by 4 & 5 *Ph.* & *Ma.c.*4.
  3. Wilful *Murther* of Malice *præpenſe*, Principal ouſt of Clergy in all caſes by *Stat.* 23 *H.* 8. *c.* 1. 25 *H.* 8. *c.* 3. 1 *E.* 6. *c.* 12.
  Acceſſory before maliciouſly, ouſted in all caſes, by 4 & 5 *Ph.* & *Ma c.*4.

4. Arſon

Clergy. 233

4. *Arson* of Houses, or Barns full of Corn, Principal ouſt of Clergy in all cafes, *viz. sur* Conviction by Verdict, or Confeſſion, by 23 *H.* 8. *c.* 1. upon ſtanding Mute, not direct anſwering, challenge above Twenty, by *Stat.* 25 *H.*8.*c.*3.

But Utlary ſtands ſubject to Clergy.

Acceſſory ouſted of Clergy in all caſes by 4 & 5 *Ph.* & *M. c.* 4.

5. Simple *Burglary*.

Principal ouſted of Clergy if utlawed, Convicted by Verdict, or Confeſſion.

Not ouſted if ſtand Mute, challenge above Twenty, or not directly anſwering.

Acceſſory before or after not ouſt of Clergy.

6. Burglary, any perſon being in the Houſe, or put in fear or dread.

Prin-

Clergy.

Principal ouſt of Clergy in all caſes, *viz.* by *Stat.* 1 *E.* 6. 12. in caſe of any Conviction or Attainder; and by 25 *H.* 8. *c.* 3. revived by 5 & 6 *E.* 6. *c.* 10. it takes away Clergy where above Twenty challenged.

But Acceſſories not ouſted of Clergy.

7. *Robbery*, which hath ſeveral Qualifications, with theſe Conſiderations:

1. From the Perſon,

Without putting in fear, but *clam & ſecrete*: By *Stat.* 8 *El. c.*4. Principal in all caſes ouſt of Clergy, Acceſſory not ouſt.

With putting in fear, Robbery in or near the High-way.

1. Principal in all caſes ouſt of Clergy, *viz.* if Appeal or Indictment by 23 *H.*8. *c.*1. Convict 23 *H.* 8. *c.* 1. Attaint 1 *E.* 6. *c.* 12. Mute, Challenge above Twenty by *Stat.* 25 *H.*8.*c.*3. revived by 5 & 6 *E.*6.*c.*10.

2. Ac-

Clergy.

2. Accessory before ouſt of Clergy in all caſes, by 4 & 5 *Ph. & Ma. c.*4.

2. From Dwelling-houſe; and this three kinds:
   1. Owner, Wife, or Servants being in the Houſe, or put in fear; here Clergy.
      1. As to to Principal, taken away by 23 *H.* 8. *c.*1. in caſe of Conviction by Verdict, or Confeſſion, and by 25 *H.* 8. *c.* 3. Revived by 5 & 6 *E.* 6. *c.* 10. in caſe of ſtanding Mute, challenge *ultra* Twenty, not directly anſwering: Alſo to a Conviction in a foreign County, if it appear by Examination not to be within Clergy in the ſame County.
      2. Acceſſory in all caſes ouſt of Clergy by *Stat.* 4 & 5 *Ph. & Ma. c.* 4.

   Notà, A Stranger in the Houſe brings it not within Statute.

2. Rob-

2. Robbing any perſon by da
or night, any perſon beir
in the ſame Houſe, and p
in fear.
Principal ouſt of Clergy l
1 E. 6. c. 12. in all caſes, b
challenging Twenty; and l
Stat. 5 & 6 E. 6. if
a foreign County Cler
upon Examination taken
way.
Acceſſories, Clergy taken aw
by 4 & 5 Ph. & Ma. c.
in all caſes.
3. Robbing any perſon in l
Dwelling Houſe, the Ow
er, his Wife, or Childr
being in any part of t
Houſe, or within the p
cincts thereof; though the
be no putting in fear. A
this extends to Booths
Fairs.
Principal ouſt of Clergy l
5 & 6 E. 6. c. 9. in ca
where the Offender is four
guilty.

Pri

Clergy.

Principal thereof in other cases shall have Clergy; as in standing Mute, challenge *ultra* Twenty.

Accessory oust by *Stat.* 4 & 5 *Ph.* & *Ma.c.*4.

4. Robbery to the value of 5 *s.* t of any Dwelling-house or Outuse thereunto belonging, though ne in the House, by *Stat.* 35 *El.*

Principal oust of Clergy in case Conviction, not of standing ute.

Accessory shall have Clergy.

Un enter in le Lodging Sir H. Hun:e *parcell de* Whitehall, *nul person :ant in Lodging, mes in autre part* Whitehall *& infreint un Chamber prist biens: Rule per advise de tices*, 1. *L' Indictment doit estre infreindre de meason de Roy vocat'* iitehall *& pur Embleer les biens* H. H. *divers persons esteant in le aon: Car nient semble al Chamber Inn de Court, lou chescun ad seve-property.* 2. *Que ceo fuit deins le* t. 5 *&* 6 E. 6. *& l'Inditement accordant.* 3. *Que in Inditement*
sur

Clergy.

fur Stat. 23 H. 8. *vel* 5 & 6 E. *doit eſtre actual breaking & au Robbery.* 4. *Que ſi laron enter meaſon le Doors open, & enfrei Chamber, & priſt biens, eſt deins* Stat. 5. E. 6. *d'ouſter luy de Clergy.*

8. *Larceny* without any of the Circumſtances.

Horſe-ſtealing ouſt of Clergy, 1 *E* 6. *c*. 12. 2 & 3 *E*. 6. 33. Princip ouſt in all caſes:

Acceſſory ouſted in no caſes.

But other Larceny, not being Ro bery nor Cut-purſe, have Clergy.

9. In *Rape*, Clergy ouſt by *St* 18 *El. c.* 7.

10. Though the Offence be wi in Clergy, yet if he had former his Clergy, and were burnt in t Hand, the *Stat.* 4 *H*. 7. *c.* 13. ouſts h of Clergy, unleſs he were a perſ in Orders, and then he muſt prod his Certificate preſently, or by time prefixed.

And ſee the *Stat.* 34 & 35 *H. c.* 14. for the manner of the Cert cate of ſuch Convictions and otl Attainders.

A

Clergy.

And though *Stat.* of 32 *H*.8. *c.* 1. hath put men in Orders in the same condition with others, in reference to Clergy; yet as to this Point of the *Stat.* 4 *H.* 7. the Clause of the *Statute* 1 *E.* 6. *c.* 12. doth give a person in Orders his Clergy the second time in all cases, but in case of, 1. Challenge above Twenty: 2. Outlary.

3. *When* Clergy shall be *allowed*.
   1. Now the use is not to put the party to challenge his Clergy till he hath pleaded, and the Inquest thereupon taken :
      1. For advantage of the party, if acquitted. ^{St.PC.f.131.}
      2. For advantage of the King for forfeiture, if Convict.
   2. It may be allowed in Discretion, though the party challenge not.
   Allowed under the Gallows, or where Judgment of *Paine fort & dure* given, or where challenge above Twenty.
   V.

Clergy.

V. *Crom. Jur.* 126. *Allow south Gallows per Just. B. R. mes nemy Gaol Delivery*: *Mes poent apres Judgment devant adjournment*, Dy.205.

Licet Ordinary retorn' non legit, & est record, & repry al autre Sessions, & tunc legit, avera benefit de ceo Dy.202. 34 H.6.49. Coron.20.

4. The *Judge*.

The Ordinary is but Minister, the Judge at Common Law is the Judge when and where to allow it, and of the Reading, 9 *E.* 4. 28. *Coron* 32.

5. What the *Effect* of Clergy allowed:

1. In ancient time the Consequen was delivery to the Ordinary, eithe to make Purgation, or *absque Purgatione*, as the case required.

But by *Stat.* 18 *El. c.*7. now only Burnt in the Hand, which hath these effects;

 1. Enables the Judge to deli
  ver him out of Prison; bu
  yet if he see cause, he may
  detain him till he find Sure
  ties of Good Behaviour.

         Anc

Clergy.

And by the *Stat.* 3 *H.* 7. *c.* 1.
If Clergy within the year, he is to be Bailed or Committed at discretion, till the year past.

2. It gives him a Capacity to purchase Goods, and retain the profits of his Lands. *Foxley's case, 5 Rep.*

But the Goods he had at the time of the Conviction are forfeit.

3. It restores him to his Credit. *Hob.* 377. *Searle's Case.*

Le Stat. 25 H. 8. *que toll Clergy del 'ersons arrain in foreign County sur 'xamination extend solement al tiels Felonies d'ont Clergy oust per Stat' 23 H. 8. & nemy per subsequent Stat. It pur ceo Rule in* Anne Coles Case: *si feme infreint meason in County de . in day time, & prist biens south value de* 10 s. *& eux import in County de* D. *& la arraigne, el serra arse n maine: quia nul mister in pavor me require per le* Stat. 23 H. 8.

Robbery de value de 10 d. & import foreign County & la arrain est Pe-

R tit

Clergy.

tit Larceny, 2 Jac. More's Rep. *quia le Stat.* 25 H. 8. *extend solement al cestuy que demand Clergy, que n'est in case de Pet' Larceny.*

Indite de Robbery in quadam via pedestri, *avera Clergy: Car le Stat. parle de Robbery* in vel prope altam viam regiam. *T.* 38 *H.*8. *More* 5.

Pleas to the Felony.

1. **D**emurrer.
2. Pleas in Abatement and Bar.
3 The General Issue.

1. For *Demurrer*.
It amounts to a Confession of the Indictment, as laid; and therefore if the Indictment good, Judgment against the Prisoner, and Execution. C. West. 1.c.12.

2. For Pleas *in Abatement*.
If Prisoner plead *Misnosmer* of his Sirname unto an Appeal, it goes in Abatement: But in case of Indictment, he shall be put to answer the Treason or Felony. St. PC. 181.
1 H.5. 5.

But Misnosmer of the Christian Names goes in Abatement; and if it be confessed by the King's Attorney, or found, the Indictment falls. 11 *H.*4.*Coron.*88.

But then he must give his true Name, and by that Name he may be forthwith Indicted.

Pleas in Bar.

Auterfoits acquit.

Auterfoits acquit:
1. If a perfon be acquitted upon an infufficient Indictment or Appeal, yet upon a new Indictment he may be arraigned for the fame Felony. 4 *R. Vaux*'s Cafe, *licet Judgment done.*

St.PC.105, 106.

2. *Auterfoits acquit* of one Felony, no Bar to an Indictment or Appeal of another Felony, &c. though committed before the Acquittal.

3. *Auterfoits acquit* as Principal, no Bar to an Indictment againſt him as Acceffory to the fame Felony after; But it feems he cannot be after indicted as Acceffory before, *Stamf.* 105.

4. In an Appeal of Death or other Felony, *Auterfoits acquit*, upon an Indictment for the fame Felony, was a good Bar in all Cafes; therefore
if

if an Appeal was pending, the Court would surcease the Arraignment of the Prisoner upon an Indictment till it was determined: Or though no Appeal pending, yet in case of death, would surcease till the year past.

But at this day *Auterfoits acquit* in an Indictment of Death no Bar to an Appeal, by *Stat.* 3 *H.*7. *c.*1. for the Prisoner, notwithstanding the Acquittal; but in other Appeals it stands a Bar to an Appeal.

5. But *Auterfoits acquit* in an Appeal, Bar to an Indictment of the same Felony.

   1. Unless the Appeal be Erroneous in substance.
   2. Or unless the Appeal be by a wrong Person.
   3. Unless the Acquittal be by Battel; for in these cases he may be indicted again.

6. He that pleads this Plea, need not have the Record *in poigne*, because it goes in Bar. 3 *E.*3. *B. Coron.* 217.

7. Though there be *Variance* between the Indictment, &c. yet if it be such as may admit an *Averment*, to be the same, yet it may be pleaded.

Variance in the *Name*, if *Conus per un Name & auter*.

Variance in the *Day* of Felony supposed to be committed.

Variance in the *Place*, but by the Opinion of 4 *H*. 5. acquit of Larceny in one County no Bar in another.

Variance in l'Offence auterfoits acquit, attaint de Murther ou Manslaughter turr' Petit Treason.

Auterfoits Convict or *Attaint.*

1. Where a Bar to the same Felony:
   1. *Auterfoits attaint* of the same Felony in an Appeal Bar to an Indictment; for the Effect is obtained, the death of the party: But *vid.* no Bar in Appeal. C.PC.213.
   2. *Auterfoits convict* by Verdict or Confession of Manslaughter in an Indictment and had Clergy, Bar in Appeal, though it be of Murther, for the Fact the same in both, though the Offences differ in degree. 4 Rep. 45. *Wigg*'s case.

Auterfoits acquit sur insufficient Enditement, & nul Judgment done, n'est plea : Mes auterment est si Judgement soit done tanque ceo reverse. *Vauxe*'s Case, 4 Rep.

2. Where a Bar to an Arraignment for another Offence.

Auterfoits Convict.

S. PC. 107.

1. *Auterfoits attaint* of Felony, is no Bar to arraign him of Treason committed before the Felony for the King's Interest.

E. PC 213.

And it seems, if the Treason was committed after the Felony, then he shall be arraigned of the Treason, for the Offence is different.

2. *Auterfoits attaint* of one Felony, Bar to an Arraignment of Felony: But this hath these *Exceptions*,

1. Where the first Attainder is pardoned, there he may be arraigned for the former Felonies, though committed before.

S. PC. 66, 107.

2. In case of Appeal he shall be arraigned at every one of their Suits, notwithstanding he be attaint at one Suit.

The like it seems upon indictment of Robbery, because by the *Stat.* the party is to have restitution.

3. *Auter-*

3. *Auterfoits convict,* and had Clergy after *Stat.* 25 *E.* 3. *c.* 5. had been a Bar to an Arraignment for another Felony, though not within Clergy. *Dy.* 214.

But now by *Stat.* 8 *El. c.* 4. after Purgation, and 18 *El. c.* 7. after burning in the Hand, he shall be put to answer former Felonies not within Clergy, or for any offence after Clergy allowed.

And Note, That he that pleads a Plea in Bar to an Indictment or Appeal that confesseth not the Felony, shall plead over to the Felony; otherwise if it confess the Felony; as Pardon, or Release.

Pardons.

Pardons.

3. **PARDONS**
Are either *of Course and Right*; such are,
1. For a person Convict of Manslaughter, or *Se defendendo*.

St.PC.102.
2. An Approver that vanquisheth the Appellee.

Pardons *of Grace*:
1. Some things requisite to their allowance *by Statute*.

1. By *Stat.* 13 *R.* 2. *c.* 1. Pardon of Murther, Rape or Treason must be especially expressed in the Pardon, otherwise it ought not to be allowed in such cases. *Vide si extend al Petit Treason & Accessories*, 22 E. 4. 19. Lam. 293.

2 By *Stat.* 10 *E* 3. *c.*2. there must be Surety of good abearing, otherwise the Charter void; but a special *Non obstante* may prevent it.

2. Matter

2. Matter *at Common Law* confiderable.

1. Charter of Pardon no Bar of an Appeal; and if the party be Utlawed in Appeal, and the King pardon, he fhall have a *Scire facias* againft the Appellor, who may pray Execution notwithftanding fuch Pardon; but if returned *Scire feci*, and appears not, then Appellee fhall upon the Pardon be difcharged.

2. Pardon of all Felonies is no Bar to Execution, if the Felon be Attaint; yet an Exception of all Burglaries excepts the Burglary for which the party is Attainted.

3. Pardon of all Attainders, not good with a pardon of the Felony.

4. The Pardon of Felony reciting in the Pardon that the party is Indicted, and in truth he is not, this is void.

5. The

Pardon.

C.P.C. 337.

5. The King may Pardon the Burning in the Hand in Appeal, & *l'Imprisonment per ceo discharge.*

6. *S'il apres infreint Peace Scire fac' gist a repealer le Pardon, & serra pendu pur primer Offence per le* Stat. 10 E. 3. 3 H. 7. 7. *viz. nisi soit non obstante le* Stat.

7. *Pardon de tout Felonies per* A. & B. *vel eor' alter' commit: pardon several,* Dy. 34. 22 E 4. 7.

Pleading the Pardon.

He that pleads a General Pardon by Parliament, wherein are Exceptions, must aver that he is none of the persons excepted.

But of a General Pardon by Parliament without Exception, the Court *ex Officio* must take notice.

He that pleads a Particular Pardon,

1. Must shew it under Seal.
2. Must have a Writ of Allowance, *qu'il ad trove Surety som'*, Stat. 10 E. 3.

Mes

Pardon. 253

Mes lou nul brief d'allowance nul mort. 5 E. 4. 132.

3. If Variance, he muſt aver that the ſame perſon.

General

General Issue.

THUS far of Pleas in Bar upon Indictments or Appeals: Now we come to *Pleas to the Fact, Not Guilty.*

1. Regularly he that pleads any Special Matter in Bar in Cases Capital, that confesseth not the Felony, notwithstanding the Plea found against him, the Felony shall be enquired of, and therefore he shall plead over to the Felony.

2. The immediate *consequent* of this Plea is *Trial*; and that is either,

By the Country.
By Peers.
By Battel.

Trial per Patriam.

1. Concerning Trial *per Patriam*; and therein,
   1. Where Issues tried.
   2. What Process against Jury.
   3. Before whom.
   4. Challenge.
   5. Evidence to be given.
   6. Verdict.

1. *Where* tried.

1. For Trial of *foreign Treasons* and foreign Accessories, or stroke in one County, and death in another, *vide supra* in Indictments.

2. For Trial of *foreign Pleas* by Stat. 22 *H.*8. *c.* 14. made perpetual by 32 *H.*8.*c.*3. Foreign Pleas pleaded by a person indicted of Felony, and Triable by the County, shall be tried where the party is Arraigned; but it is now in Treason triable in the foreign County by virtue of Stat. 1 & 2 *Ph.* & *Ma. c.*

2. *Pro.*

2. *Process against the Jury.*

1. *Nota*, The Justices of Gaol Delivery have their Pannel returned by the Sheriff, without any Precept, by a bare Award; but Justices of Oyer and Terminer not.

2. By good *Opinion*, the Justices of Peace, or Oyer and Terminer, cannot make their *Venire facias* to try an Issue retornable the same Sessions; but Justices of Gaol Delivery clearly may.

St.PC.f.155.   3. If several persons Arraigned upon an Indictment or Appeal, and they severally plead Not Guilty, the Plaintiff may take out one *Venire facias*, or several.

4. If the *Venire facias* be joynt, Challenge by one drawn against all.

Crom. 100.   5. Though Pannel be joynt, and *Tales* awarded, yet Court of Gaol Delivery may after sever the Pannel to prevent that inconvenience.

6. In

6. In Appeal, if after Issue Plaintiff tries it not, a *Venire* by *Proviso* may be for the Defendant; yet upon that *Venire* Plaintiff may have a *Tales*.

3. *Tales*.

1. If a full Jury appear not, or be challenged in Indictment or Appeal, the Plaintiff may have a *Tales*.

2. Upon Indictment or Appeal, because Defendant may Challenge peremptorily, *Tales* may be granted larger than the Principal Pannel, as forty *Tales*, 14 *H*.7.7.

3. But the succeeding *Tales* must be less than the former, unless the first be quashed, and then the same number with that which is quashed.

4. If any of the Jury die before sworn, a new *Tales* grantable.

3. *Before whom?*

1. A *Nisi prius* not grantable where the King Party, unless prayed by his Attorney.
2. By *Stat.* 14 *H.* 6. *c.* Power to Justices of *Nisi prius* to give Judgment in Felony and Treason tried before them.
3. By *Stat.* 42 *E.* 3. *c.* 11. Enquest in Assise and Gaol Delivery may be taken before the Pannel returned in Court, but not in other Cases.

Challenge.

4. *Challenge* of Array or Polls.

1. *Ex parte Regis,* by *Stat.* 33 *E.* 1. *c.* the King shall not Challenge without Cause; but yet he is not compellable to shew the Cause till the Pannel perused.

2. *Ex parte prisonarii,* the Challenge is either Peremptory, or upon Cause.

1. *Peremptory* Challenge.

1. A Peremptory Challenge not allowable, but where the life of a Prisoner comes in question, and therefore not upon Collateral Issues.

2. At Common Law he might have challenged peremptorily 35 under three full Juries; and if he challenged above, he should have Judgment to be hanged, 3 *H.* 7. 12.

But by *Stat.* 22 *H* 8. *c.* 4. made perpetual, by 32 *H.* 8. *c.* 3. it is reduced to 20; and now if he Challenge above 20, he shall not be therefore hanged, or forfeit, but his

Chal-

Challenge.

C. PC. 227. Challenge Over-ruled, and he put upon his Trial; yet *vid. Statutes, semble contra.*

3. In cafe of Treafon and Petit Treafon, the Challenge of 35 reftored by *Stat.* 1 & 2 *Ph.* & *M. c.* 10.

2. Challenge *for Caufe*; we mention but three;
1. Caufe of *Infufficiencies.* By the *Stat.* 2 *H.* 5. *c.* 3. 40 *s. per Ann.* required in County; but this, as to Aliens, corrected by 8 *H.* 6. *c. ult.* in Cities by *Stat.* 23 *H.*8. *c.* 13. Goods to the value of 40 *l.*
2. *Unindifferency.*
Indictor not to be of Jury by *Stat.* 25 *E.* 3. *c.* 3.
3. In reference to an *Alien,* & *medietat' linguæ,* where
   1. In no cafe Indictors ought to be *de medietate linguæ.*
   2. In Treafon trial *per medietat' linguæ* repel *per Stat'* 1 & 2 *Ph.* & *Ma. que ad repel* 28 *E.* 3. in that cafe.

3. In

3. In Appeal by an Alien against an Alien, no *medietat' linguæ*.
4. Scot no Alien, to have *Medietatem linguæ*.
5. The Jurors need not be of the same Nation, but any Aliens.
6. He that will have advantage of Trial *per medietatem linguæ* must pray it, otherwise he cannot have benefit by way of Challenge, *Dy.* 304, 357.
7. *Egyptians* excluded from the Trial *per* 1 & 2 *Ph. & Ma. c.* 4.

S 3   *Evidence*

Evidence.

5. **E**vidence to the Petit Jury.
   1. In cafe of *Treafon*,
There muft be two Accufers or Witneffes by *Stat.* 1 *E.* 6. *c.* 12. & 5 *E.*6. *c.* 11. and this notwithftanding *Stat.* 1 & 2 *Ph.* & *Ma. c.*11. but only in cafe of Treafon for Counterfeiting Coin.

Thefe Witneffes muft not be only by hear-fay.

2. In cafe of *Felony*.
   1. What allowed as Evidence:
      1. By *Stat.* 1 & 2 *Ph.* & *Ma. c.* 13. & 2 & 3 *Ph.* & *Ma: c.*10. the Juftice hath power to Examine the Offender and Informer.
      2. The Examination of the Offender not upon Oath, but Subfcribed by him.
      3. Examination of others muft be upon Oath.
      4. This muft be certified by the Juftices.

1. If

Evidence.

1. If it be but a small Felony, to the Sessions.
2. If it be a great Felony, &c. to the next Gaol Delivery.
5. These Examinations, if the party be dead or absent, may be given in Evidence.

But Prudence to have the Justice or his Clerk sworn to the truth of the Examinations.

6. But Examinations, taken upon a Cause of Divorce for a forcible Marriage, not allowed to be read upon an Indictment upon 3 *H.* 7. for the same Marriage.

2. By whom.
   1. *Wife*, or her Examination, not to be used for or against her Husband. ^{Dalt.c.111.}
   2. The Examination of an *Infant* of Thirteen, nay, of Nine allowed in some cases.
   3. One Attaint of Conspiracy, Forgery, or Perjury, not allowed a Witness.
   4. One duly set on Pillory. C.P.C.219.

Evidence.

3. In what manner.
   1. Evidence for the King always upon Oath.

C,PC. c.22. But Evidence for the Prisoner not upon Oath; yet no known Law that restrains it: But by some *Statutes* in some cases, Evidence for the Prisoner upon Oath, as 31 *El.c.*4. 4 *Jac.c.*1.
The Confession of the Offender taken upon Examination, Evidence with Oath not of the Informer.

4. Where Evidence maintains the Indictment.
   1. If the Indictment be of a Felony, &c. at one *day*, though the Evidence be of another day, the Jury may find generally against Prisoner, and leave the person that is interessed in point of time

C.PC. §.230. to falsify: Or the Jury may find the true day upon their Verdict, and then the forfeiture shall relate thither.

   3. If the Indictment lay the Felony at one *place*, the Evidence proving the Fact at another place

Evidence. 265

in the same County, maintains the Indictment.

3. If the Indictment and Evidence differ in *specie mortis*, then it maintains it not: as Indictment of Poisoning, Evidence of Stabbing maintains it not.
But if the Indictment be of poysoning with one kind of Poison, and the Evidence of another; or of killing with a Dagger, and the Evidence is of killing with a Staff, yet it maintains the Indictment; for it agrees in substance and kind. C.PC.135.

9 Rep. Mackally's case.

The like of Accessories before, though the Poison or Weapon different.

4. Indictment that *A*. gave the mortal blow, and *B. C.* and *D.* were *præsentes & abbettantes*; Evidence that *B.* gave the blow, and *A. C.* and *D. præsentes & abbettantes*, yet it maintains the Indictment.

5. Indictment of *A.* as Accessory to *B* and *C.* Evidence proves him Accessory only to *B.* maintains the Indictment. 9 Rep. Sanchar's case.

6. In-

6. Indictment of Murther, *ex malitia præcogitata*; Evidence of malice in Law, as killing an Officer, or without Provocation, yet maintains the Indictment.
7. Indictment upon *Statute* of Stabbing, 21 *Jac.* Evidence that the Dead ſtrook firſt, yet Evidence to maintain the Indictment for Manſlaughter generally, *H*.23 *Car. Horwood's* Caſe.
8. Two indicted as Principals, Evidence proves one Acceſſory before, he ſhall be diſcharged of that Indictment, 26 *H*.8.5.
9. *Vid. Stat.* 21 *Jac. c.*27. Mother endeavouring to conceal the death of her Baſtard-child, ſhall ſuffer death as in caſe of Murther, unleſs ſhe prove by one Witneſs that the Child was born dead.

Vid. Act. 17 *Car. in fine*, for the farther relief of His Majeſty's Army in the Northern parts. Act continued till end of next Seſſions; continued over till ſome Act of Parliament for their continuance or diſcontinuance.

Verdict.

Verdict.

6. Verdict in cases Capital.
    1. It must be given, and the Jury cannot be discharged till it be given. St.PC.165.
    2. It must be given openly in Court, and no privy Verdict.
    3. It may be found Specially; as an Indictment of Murther, the Jury may find him Guilty,
        1. Of Manslaughter:
        2. *Per Infortunium:*
        3. *Se defendendo.*

But then they must find the manner of it, that the Court may judge thereof; so for the value or the manner of the Larceny.

Trial by Battel, Peers.

Now we should come to Trial,
    By Battel.
    By Peers: *Vid.* the whole Process thereof, *C.Pl.Cor.*27.

Judg-

Judgments in the several Cases.

I. IN High Treason:

C. PC. 218, 219.

1. In all Cases, except Counterfeiting Coin, Drawn, Hang'd, Entrails taken out and burnt, Head cut off, Body quartered, Head and Quarters hang'd up.

2. In Counterfeiting Coin, Drawn and Hang'd: *Issint per tonsure.* Dy. 230.

But the Judgment of a Woman in those cases, Drawn and Burnt.

II. In Petit Treason:

1. For a Man, Drawn and Hang'd.
2. For a Woman, Drawn and Burnt.

III. In Felony.

Hang'd till Dead: And this cannot be by the King altered to Beheading.

IV.

IV. *In Petit Larceny.*

To be Whipt.
He forfeits Goods.

V. *Death per infortunium.*

No exprefs Judgment; yet forfeits Goods.

VI. *Death Se defendendo.*

No exprefs Judgment; yet forfeits Goods.

VII. *Mifprifion of Treafon.*

Forfeits Goods; forfeits Profits of Land during Life; perpetual Imprifonment.
Vide for Seifure of Goods.
   1. Not before Indictment.
   2. Nor removed before Attainder, 1 *R.*3. *c.*3.

Falsifying Attainders.

1. By the Party, by *Writ of Error.*
2. By others *Falsifying* it.
    1. A Purchaser may falsifie an Attainder of the Vendor by Utlary or Confession in the point, if he purchase before the Attainder, and after the time of the Felony supposed
    2. A Purchaser *Mesne* between the time of the Felony committed, and the Attainder by Verdict, cannot falsifie in the point of the Offence, but he may for the time.
    3. If the Attainder was by such as had no good Commission, the Party himself may falsify the Attainder. *Casus Com. Leicest.*
    4. If the Principal attainted, and then the Accessory and Principal reverse the Attainder, the Attainder of the Accessory is *eo ipso* avoided, and his heirs may have *Mortdanc'* against the Lord by *Escheat.*
    5. Attain-

5. Attaint of Treason, and then the Treason is pardoned by Act of Parliament, the party or his Heir shall falsify Attainder.

6. In Case of *Goods*.

1. *Fugam fecit* found by the Coroner cannot be falsified, though upon his Arraignment it be found he did not fly: But if the Indictment be void or insufficient, no Forfeiture.

2. A man indicted before Justices of Oyer and Terminer, acquit by Verdict, and found he fled, and the particulars of his Goods found, they may be Traversed. St.PC.184.

3. Default till *Exigent*, though after acquitted, Goods forfeited; for it is a *fugam fecit* in Law.

But if the Indictment, Appeal, or Process insufficient, the Forfeiture saved; so if it be reversed by Error, or pardoned before *Exigent*.

Nota, Flight or *Exigent* in case of Petit Larceny, forfeits Goods.

Execution and Reprieve.

<small>C. PC. 212, 217.</small>

1. THe Execution muſt be purſuant to the Judgment, and cannot be altered by the King, as from Beheading to Hanging.

2. But King may pardon part of the Execution; as in Treaſon, he may pardon all but Beheading.

3. It muſt be done by the proper Officer.

<small>C.PC. c.7. 217. St.PC.f.198.</small>

4. If a Woman, Convict of Treaſon or Felony, be quick with Child, ſhe ſhall have one Reprieve, but not a ſecond time.

An

An Alphabetical Table of the Principal Matters of the Book.

A

Abjuration, *ousted*, 228.
    Accessory, who, 215. *before*, 217. *after*, 218. *arraignment*, 221.
Affray, 135.
Ale houses, 147.
Appeal, where prosecuted, 179. *of what matters*, 180. *of Death*. 181. *of Robbery*, 184. *of Rape*, 186. *Process in Appeal*, 187. *Court in Appeal*, 187. *Pleas in Appeal*, 189, 190.
Approver, what, 192. *who may be*, ibid. *in what cases*, 193. *of what offences*, 193. *before whom*, 194. *how demeasned*, 194. *Process*, 196. *Proceeding, upon trial*, 196. *after Trial*, 197.

An Alphabetical Table.

Arraignment, in what manner, 212. where, ibid. *of Principal and Accessory*, 213, 221.
Arrest, by a private person, commanded by Law, 89. *permitted*, 91. *by Officer*, 92.
Arson, 85.
Auterfoits acquit, 244.
   Convict, 247.

B

Ail what, 96. *in what cases*, 97. *by whom*, 103. virtute brevis, *ib*. ex officio, 104.
Barretry.
Breach of Peace, 135.
 of Prison, 87. v. *Rumper-Prison.*
Bribery.
Bridges, 143.
Burglary, 79.
Burning, Arson, 85.

C

Hallenge, 259.
 Champerty, 151.
Chance medley, 31.

     Clergy,

An Alphabetical Table.

Clergy, 229.
Clipping Mony, 19.
Coin, Treason concerning it, ibid.
Commitment, 94.
Concealment of Felony, 129.
      by Juries, ibid.
Coroner, 170.
Counterfeiting Coin, 19. *Great Seal,* 18.
Courts, 156.

D

D*Eceit and Cozenage.*
  Demurrer, 243
Deodand, 33.
Drunkenness, 149.

E

E*Scape, in the party,* 111. *in a Stranger,* 112. *in an Officer,* 133.
Evidence, 262.
Execution, 272.
Extortion.

An Alphabetical Table.

F

F*Alsifying Attainder, &c.* 270.
Felo de se, 28
Felony by Common Law, 26.
    by Statute, 117.
Forcible Entry, 138.
    Detainer, 139.
Forfeiture.
Forgery, 151.
Forestalling, 152.

G

G *Aol Delivery,* 158.
  General Issue, 254.

H

H *Eresie,* 3.
  High-ways, 144.
Homicide, per Infortunium, 31. *ex necessitate,* 35. *in execution of Justice,* 35. *in advancement of Justice,* 36. *upon private Interest, Justifiable,* 39. *Excusable,* 41.
Hue and Cry, 90.

I

An Alphabetical Table.

I

Imprisonment, vide *Arrest*.
Indictment, where requisite, 198. by whom, 201. of what matters, 203. before whom, 205. the form, 206. proof, 208.
Ingrossing, 152.
Inns, 146.
Judgment, in several cases, 268.
Jurisdictions, 156
Jury, vide *Process & Challenge*.
Justices of *Assize*, 164.
  of *Peace*, 165.

L

Larceny, Simple, 60. Mixt, 71. from the person, ibid. from the house, 76.
Leet, 175.

M

An Alphabetical Table.

M

M *Aihem*, 133.
Malice, 44.
Manslaughter, 56.
Medietas Linguæ, 260.
Misnosmer, 243.
Misprisions, 126 *Negative, of Treason*, 127. *of Felony*, 129. *Positive*, 131.
Mittimus, 94.
Murther, 43.
Mute, 225. *what standing mute*, ibid. *the consequence*, 226.

N

N *Usances*, 134 143.

O

O *Ffences, the kinds*, 1. *against God*, 3. *against Man, Capital*, 9. *not Capital*, 126. *of Inferiour nature*, 134. *by Statute*, 151.
Oyer and Terminer, 161.

An Alphabetical Table.

P.

P*Aine fort & dure,*225.
*Pardon of Courſe,*250. *of Grace,* ibid. *Pleading,*252.
*Perjury,*151.
*Piracy,*77.
Pleas, Declinatory, 228. *to the Felony,* 243. *in Abatement,* ibid. *in Bar,*244.
Preſent.
*Principal and Acceſſory,*215. *Arraignment,*221.
*Priſon,*107.
Proceſs, upon Appeals and Indictments 209. *againſt Jury,*256.
*Provocation,*57.

R

R*Eligion,* 153.
*Reſcue,*116.
*Reſtitution,*140.
Riding armed.
*Riot,*137.
*Robbery,*71.
*Rumper Priſon,*107.

S

An Alphabetical Table.

S

Sanctuary, *ousted*, 228.
Se *defendendo*, 41.
Sheriff, 173. his Turn, ibid.
Subornation, 151.

T

Tales, 257.
Theft bote, 130.
Tipling, 147.
Treason, High Treason, 9.
Petit Treason, 23.
Trial, per Patriam, 255. by Battel, by Peers, 267.
Turn of the Sheriff, 173.

V

Verdict, 267.

W

Witchcraft, 6.

THE END.

www.ingramcontent.com/pod-product-compliance
Lightning Source LLC
Chambersburg PA
CBHW032047230426
43672CB00009B/1499